MEEKER —

THE STORY OF THE MEEKER MASSACRE
AND THE THORNBURGH BATTLE
September 29, 1879

by Fred H. Werner

Published by

Werner Publications
2020 18th Avenue
Greeley, Colorado 80631

OTHER BOOKS BY FRED H. WERNER

Before the Little Big Horn   (Revised Edition,
                                    Greeley, Colorado - 1983)

The Slim Buttes Battle   (Greeley, Colorado - 1981)

The Dull Knife Battle   (Greeley, Colorado - 1981)

The Soldiers Are Coming   (Greeley, Colorado - 1982)

Faintly Sounds The War-Cry   (Greeley, Colorado - 1983)

Greeley Printing Co.

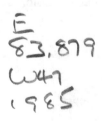

93857

ACKNOWLEDGEMENTS

The help a writer receives from various individuals, in gathering the information necessary to publish a book of this nature, is invaluable. First and foremost among the people I need to recognize and thank is Bill Squire of the Willow Bend Ranch, near Meeker, Colorado. Most of the Thornburgh Battle area is located on the Squire Ranch.

Bill and his wife, as well as son Jeff, accorded me their sincere hospitality and cooperation during my many trips to their ranch, to conduct the field research.

I would also like to express my appreciation and thanks to the following, who also cooperated with me in carrying out my research of the Meeker and Thornburgh Battle:

Mr. and Mrs. Doug Wellman & son John — Meeker, Colorado.

Aaron Woodward — Meeker, Colorado

Hartley Bloomfield — Meeker, Colorado

Francis McKee — Meeker, Colorado

Iva Kendall and Staff of White River Museum — Meeker, Colorado

Dan Seely — Meeker, Colorado

Esther Fromm and Staff of Greeley Public Library

Greeley Municipal Museum — Greeley, Colorado

John Wheeler — Greeley, Colorado

Dr. John Fulbright — Greeley, Colorado

Arlen Horn — Greeley, Colorado

Colorado Historical Society — Denver, Colorado

Wyoming State Historical Society — Cheyenne, Wyoming

The National Archives — Washington, D.C.

TABLE OF CONTENTS

PART ONE

PART TWO

Recent Research At The Thornburgh Battle Site and Meeker
Massacre Site

Introduction

CHAPTER ONE

Meeker — An Enigma

Nathan C. Meeker will go down in history as an individual who was understood by very few people. Some of his closest friends, while respecting his honesty and dedication of purpose, were often " turned off " by his sometimes brusque and abrupt manner. He was well-read in many fields, but was especially knowledgeable in the agricultural field. His vision of an ideal society was far in advance of his contemporaries. That may have been one of the reasons for people misunderstanding him.

Meeker was born in Euclid, (near Cleveland) Ohio, in 1814. He was married to Arvilla D. Smith in April of 1844. After a varied career in a number of fields, Meeker became interested in establishing an ideal community, somewhere in the far West. He had been employed by the New York Tribune and one of his assignments was to write an article on Utah's Kingdom of the Deseret.

He took the train to make the trip but was brought to a halt near Ft. Steele, in Wyoming, due to a heavy November snowstorm. He changed his travel plans and turned eastward at Cheyenne, Wyoming. He visited the area near the junction of the South Platte and the Cache la Poudre rivers.

He was quite impressed with the possibilities of the region and came up with a new plan - a "Union Colony of Colorado." He envisioned "temperance people of good moral character, " who wanted a less restrictive life. Each person would be asked to give $145 towards a fund for the purchase of a large tract of fertile land in the Colorado Rockies area. Each member would be permitted to buy up to 160 acres of farm land, near the town, as will as a lot in town. Surplus land would be sold and the funds used for a Colony irrigation system, schools, and a cattle herd. A cooperative system for washing clothes, baking bread, and wholesale buying, would also be set up.

Meeker's wife Arvilla, at first objected to leaving their home in New York and also risking their entire savings of $10,000 in the Union Colony plan. She finally agreed, providing Meeker would give up his habit of chewing tobacco. This he agreed to do - in fact, he became very much opposed to the use of tobacco in any form, after he gave up the habit.

Horace Greeley, editor of the New York Tribune, approved of the plan. He was a staunch supporter of Meeker and a good friend. With Greeley's approval, Meeker issued a notice in the Tribune on

Horace Greeley, editor of the New York Tribune, was of great assistance to his friend, Nathan C. Meeker, in establishing the Union Colony — later named Greeley, in his honor.

Courtesy Greeley Municipal Museum

December 14, 1869 - calling for "temperance people of good moral character" to sign up for the proposed Union Colony.

A meeting was subsequently held on December 23, at Cooper Union. The room was filled with men from all parts of the country. Meeker was introduced to the assemblage by Greeley. Meeker told the crowd that one of the locations he had in mind was "well-watered with streams and springs, dotted with pine groves and with an abundance of coal and stone." He also stressed temperance, religious tolerance, and education, as important in making the Union Colony a cultural model for all the world to see and admire.

A location committee was chosen and a site selected. By spring of 1870, some 200 colonists had flocked to the "promised land." Sad to relate however, instead of "pine groves sheltered by majestic mountains," they found a barren, treeless plain, located along the banks of the Cache la Poudre River. It is said that fifty of the colonists, upon arriving at the site and surveying the treeless plain, immediately took the next train for home. Apparently, Meeker's Utopia was not for them.

Some of the settlers discovered that Meeker held them in low esteem because he considered them to have loose morals. Older settlers referred to the newcomers as "the Saints," and called the founder, "Father Meeker" - in a derogatory manner.

Although the colonists wanted to name the new town in honor of Meeker, he insisted that it be called Greeley, in honor of his good friend and benefactor. The colonists held Meeker in high esteem in spite of his many mistakes. He was a tireless worker and it is said that once his friends had to put him to bed because they were afraid he would kill himself working. He devoted all of his efforts to the welfare and growth of the colony as well as his life's savings. Many times he spent his own funds for colony expenses, forgetting to collect from the colony's treasurer - his friend, Horace Greeley.

In order to bolster the faith of the colonists in the future of the town, Meeker built the most expensive home in Greeley. It was located on the corner of Plum and Monroe Streets, half-a-mile from the center of town. Author's Note - This house still stands in Greeley today and is a National Historical Site, known as The Meeker Home. It is located at 1324 - 9th Avenue. Meeker borrowed $1,000 from Horace Greeley in 1870, to start the Greeley Tribune newspaper which is still in existence today.

Meeker kept up a steady flow of articles dealing with the Colony which he sent to his friend Greeley for publication in the New York Tribune. The money he received from this source was

Nathan C. Meeker was one of the prime movers in the establishment of the Union Colony, which was later named Greeley, in honor of his friend and benefactor, Horace Greeley.

not enough to keep him going so he continued borrowing from Greeley, with the understanding that he would repay his debts when financially able to do so.

Fate now stepped in to alter Meeker's plans and as we shall see, his entire future. Horace Greeley became ill and died on November 29, 1872. Not long after, Meeker was notified by the new ownership of the New York Tribune that his articles on Colorado would no longer be accepted. In addition, the executor of Greeley's estate informed Meeker that Greeley had died practically broke. Greeley's two daughters, Ida and Gabrielle, needed the money that Meeker owed their father and the executor advised Meeker to pay the $1,000 owed to the Greeley estate or face possible court action.

Meeker's troubles were further compounded when the Christian Union paper held him liable for several hundred dollars which the paper had loaned another colonist. Additionally, as problems developed for the colonists, they blamed Meeker for their troubles. The colonists experienced grasshopper plagues, lack of normal rainfall, and other misfortunes.

During these trying times some of Meeker's worst traits surfaced. He became more brusque and tactless than ever. He preached endlessly about the sins of drinking, gambling, smoking, and laziness. He insulted some of his friends by berating them in public. He seemed to go out of his way to be obnoxious and unpleasant.

Meeker also continued to be hounded by Charles Storrs of New York, the executor of the Greeley estate. He received a letter from Storrs during the winter of 1877, in which Meeker was threatened with legal proceedings if the $1,000 debt was not paid. Meeker was determined to pay the debt and made a trip to Denver to consult with Bela M. Hughes, a prominent Denver attorney. He intended asking Hughes to see about getting him a job as Agent at a Colorado Indian Agency. This type of job paid only about $1,500 a year but the expenses were small. If he could get an agency job, Meeker felt he could pay off the debt within two years.

Hughes was rather pessimistic about Meeker's chances as an Indian Agent. But in April 1877, he wrote Meeker that there might possibly be an opening at the White River Ute Agency in Colorado. Nothing further was heard from Hughes during 1877. But early in 1878, Meeker received a letter from Senator Teller, in which he mentioned an interview with the Commissioner of Indian Affairs, Edward A. Hayt. The interview concerned Meeker's request for a job as Indian agent.

Not long after, Meeker received word that his name had been submitted to the Senate, as Indian Agent for the White River Agency. On March 18, 1878, Meeker's appointment was confirmed. The long period of waiting was finally over and now Meeker busied himself with preparations during April, for the trip to the White River Agency. He discovered that the Agency was located 185 miles south of the Union Pacific station at Rawlins.

Meeker had been instructed to select a staff for the Agency and he interviewed young Greeley men for the positions available. He seemed to be living in an euphoric heaven and pictured the Ute Indians not as a problem but as a barbaric people who would welcome him with open arms. He would lead them from sin to a new life of Christian virtues and self-sustenance in their daily living, At age sixty-one, Meeker literally took on a new lease on life. He was facing a new challenge and he accepted it with confidence and grim determination.

Nathan Meeker left Greeley on May 3, 1878, for the White River Ute Indian Agency. It was a chilly morning as he said good-bye to his family at the Greeley depot, headed for Cheyenne. His wife Arvilla and daughter Josephine were to join him at the Agency later. He planned to stay at the Agency for only about two years - only long enough to pay off his debt to the Horace Greeley family. Josephine, or Josie as he called her, was to be hired as a teacher and physician, at $65.00 per month. Arvilla would act as postmistress and other duties at the Agency. Josie would also run a boarding house for the Agency employees and they would be charged $2.50 per week.

Meeker's first trip to the Agency was one of an exploratory nature. The former Agent had been Rev. E. H. Danforth, and Meeker wanted to acquaint himself with the situation at the Agency as well as to pay off the former employees. Meeker was accompanied by his good friend William H. Post. Post had been secretary for the Union Colony but had returned to his former home in New York. When he was offered a job as Agency clerk, he was happy to accept.

The two men traveled by rail to Fort Steele and then to Rawlins, Wyoming. Here Meeker met James France. This man owned a store in Rawlins and also held contracts with the Interior Department to haul Ute Indian supplies to the White River Agency. He informed Meeker that the Utes were in a very bad mood due to the year's supply of annuity goods being held at Rawlins, because the contractor had failed to pay the Union Pacific freight bill. In fact, the Indians hadn't received any rations or annuities during all of 1877. In addition, the Indian Bureau owed the Utes $112,000 for the San Juan cessions and some other lands given up by the Utes.

France further informed Meeker that two of the White River Ute bands, under Chiefs Jack and Douglas, had almost starved during the last winter. They were forced to look for game in Wyoming and in the Bear and Little Snake valleys in order to find enough food to exist. According to France, the situation at the agency itself was very bad. The previous agent, Rev. Danforth, had apparently met with little success in getting the Utes to live in houses and learn to farm.

After France had briefed Meeker on the entire situation he closed by advising Meeker to take the first train back to Greeley. He said that the Utes could stage an uprising at any time, due to the existing situation. He also informed Meeker that the two principal White River Chiefs, Douglas and Jack, would be difficult to work with. They had already heard that Meeker would bear down on them and carry out the government's program of insisting that the Indians learn to work and become self-sustaining.

Meeker patiently heard France out but he was so confident in his own abilities that he was certain the Utes would respond to kindess and love. He pictured himself as a leader who would show the Indians a better way of life and they would respond by following him from darkness into light. The White River Agency would be another shining example of Meeker's converting unproductive land into fertile production and habitation - such was Meeker's belief.

Meeker and Post continued their journey, arriving at the Agency in May, 1878. What they saw had a very depressing effect on them. The Agency consisted of a number of small buildings with dirt roofs and appeared to be in such poor condition that they could collapse at any time. Meeker's spirits were momentarily dampened as he surveyed the scene. Surely this was not the end of the road for him. He was determined to make his newest venture a success, no matter what the odds or the cost.

Nothing daunted, Meeker pitched in with his usual enthusiasm and soon righted some of the mistakes that had been made at the Agency. He received invaluable assistance from Secretary of the Interior, Carl Schurz, in seeing that the Ute annuities of 1877 were forthcoming. Flour, oats, and plug tobacco were now distributed on a weekly basis under the supervision of William Post, the new Agency clerk. Mail service between the Agency and Rawlins was also speeded up.

Chief's Douglas and Johnson were both impressed by Meeker's prompt attention and solution of the Agency problems.

Arvilla D. Meeker came to the Union Colony with her husband and later joined him at the White River Indian Agency.

Sketch by Jack Henderson

Chief Jack did not respond as favorably, however. When Meeker told him that Jack's band would be taught how to milk cows and become rich like the white man, Jack said that he and his band would rather remain Indians and continue their hunting lifestyle. He felt that with the annuities and money the Indians would receive from the government, they were already rich. Meeker quietly listened to Chief Jack's comments but secretly resolved that Jack would be taught that the Agent would give the orders and they must be obeyed by the Indians.

Meeker noted that about twelve miles below the Agency, an area of beautiful pasture-land stretched out on which the Ute ponies grazed. This area was called Powell Park and was some five hundred feet lower than the present location of the Agency. It was warmer there in the winter and generally free of snow as well. Some 2,000 Ute ponies grazed in Powell Park. Meeker envisioned the 10,000 acre area as land suitable for irrigation and crop-raising. There was also a racetrack located there which belonged to Chief Johnson. Meeker now realized that the ponies were essential to the Indian way of life and that if he were to succeed in making farmers out of the Utes, the ponies must go. He was firmly convinced that he could reason with the Utes and get them to change over to the white men's ways.

In order to get his grandiose plan launched, Meeker wrote to Secretary Schurz for an initial amount of $20,000. This would be used to start a model farm, laying out and digging a ditch to irrigate the crop lands in Powell Park, and fencing the farm. He would fence a sufficient acreage which would allow the work horses, milk cows, and beef cattle to graze inside of a fenced compound. His plans also called for moving the Agency from its present up-river location to the Powell Park farm complex.

Meeker had many other future projects in mind but was satisfied that his intial request would get things going. The other would come later. Secretary Schurz gave his consent to the request and Meeker set out in July of 1878 to purchase farm machinery and to hire qualified workers for the projects. He returned to Greeley and while there, learned that Arvilla and Josie were leaving for the Agency. Arrangements had been made for them to take the train to Rawlins and from there they would be transported to the agency by way of a four-mule wagon, driven by Joe Collum.

In Greeley, Meeker found that more than a hundred young men were waiting to apply for jobs at the Agency. He engaged John S. Titcomb to lay out the proposed canal. Ed Clark was hired because of his knowledge of lumber. He also hired Fred Williams,

Josephine Meeker, affectionately called Josie by her father, joined her father at the Agency and served in the capacity as cook for the employes as well as teacher for the Ute children.

John Dunbar, and Ed Mansfield to build roads and bridges. Others whom he considered were Arthur Thompson, Harry Dresser, and Fred Shepard.

Meeker was very pleased with the reception the people of Greeley gave him. Not too long ago, many had avoided him due to his criticism of many of the colonists. Now, it was a different story. He had a good job as Indian Agent and he also had $20,000 to spend on supplies, clothing, machinery, etc., as well as money for hiring a staff. Things definitely had taken on a rosier hue for Meeker.

Meeker and Engineer Titcomb left for the Agency and were driven there by Joe Collum who met them at Rawlins. As they neared the Agency, they were met by a drum-beating, happy crowd of Utes, who welcomed them to the Agency. As Meeker and Titcomb drove over Yellow Jcket Pass and down Coal Creek Canyon, the sun was slowly setting as they reached the Agency. To Meeker, it seemed that he was home once again - this time in strange surroundings, but nevertheless home.

Meeker and his wife Arvilla became concerned with the way Josie adapted herself to Agency life. She was a friend to all to the Utes and although she had been hired to teach the Ute children, sympathized with the parents in their stand about school. Ute parents were afraid that educating their children would break up their family ties, since the children would then go out into the world instead of remaining with the tribe. She also participated in many Ute activities, with evident joy.

For Meeker himself, it was a very interesting experience since there were so many things to write about. All during the summer and fall of 1878, he spent many hours writing letters to Commissioner Hayt of the Indian Bureau; to Senator Teller, William Byers, and to Pitkin - the Colorado Governor-elect. Several letters were also written to Major Thornburgh, commandant at Fort Steele, requesting his assistance in keeping Chief Jack's band from leaving the Agency to roam in Wyoming, for several months at a time. This request went unheeded - or at least, unanswered.

The newly-employed engineer, Titcomb, serveyed a route for the projected canal and digging was begun by a Mr. Lithcomb of Bear River. Chief Douglas and his band were employed to help finish the first mile of the canal. They were paid wages plus double rations. The young men who had been hired in Greeley, plowed and planted forty acres of winter wheat. Sagebrush was cleared away to make way for streets in the new Agency complex. Douglas Avenue ran west while Ute Avenue ran north. The Agency office and house were to be built at the southeast corner of Ute and Douglas Avenues. A bunkhouse was built for the employees as well as a boarding house and living quarters. Near the bunkhouse, a storeroom and a blacksmith shop were re-assembled from the material obtained at the old agency buildings.

Meeker was very high in his praise of Johnson, who was a brother-in-law of Chief Ouray. Meeker had this to say about Johnson in an article published in the Greely Tribune:

"Some of the men planted potatoes last spring. The one who is making most of them is Johnson, a considerable Chief, and one who takes the lead in progress and enterprise. He is not given to politics at all and he devotes his energies to improving his domestic affairs. He has three cows from which he has milk, butter, and cheese; and poultry and goats. A table has been made for him at which he and his eat. He has crockery, dishes, and if he had a house he would probably make things shine. Susan, Johnson's wife, is a good genius and she makes her husband do as she bids. She is a large, handsome woman, reminding one of that Boston lady, Louise Chandler Moulton. (Mrs. Moulton, a friend of Meeker's when both wrote for the New York Tribune, presided for years over a Boston literary salon.)

At some point during this period, Meeker became quite interested in Arvilla's housemaid, Jane. She was a beautiful girl, about Josie's age. She was married to a Ute named Pauvitz. Her husband's brother, Antelope, was a sub-chief and had some influence in the tribe. Meeker tried for some months to cultivate her friendship, hoping to establish a link in the communications between himself and his Ute charges. Instead, Jane turned out to be a carrier of gossip from the discontented employes to Douglas and Jack. Some of the Agency employes felt they were being driven too hard in the establishment and development of Father Meeker's Utopia.

Finding that Jane was a capricious young woman inclined to flirting with others and belittling Meeker's stature as a man, he decided to curry her favor no longer. He became involved in a heated conversation with her and she walked out on him, heading for the Chief Douglas lodge. It was then that Meeker realized he had said some things that he shouldn't have, during his conversation with her. In order to let Jane know who was "the boss", Meeker said that the Utes didn't own the White River Valley and furthermore, they could only stay there as long as they did his bidding. He now realized that he had committed a very serious blunder — one which would come back to haunt him and in the end, hasten his destruction.

Major T.T. Thornburgh received several letters from Agent Meeker, requesting assistance in keeping the White River Utes on their reservation, during the summer months.

Courtesy of National Anthropological Archives,

Smithsonian Institution

CHAPTER TWO

The Storm Clouds Gather

After some thought, Meeker decided to write an article for publication in the Greely Tribune. In this article, he detailed his conversation with Jane. The article was read by William B. Vickers, who had been an editor of the Colorado Sun in the early days of Greeley. Vickers subscribed to the doctrine that "The Utes Must Go!" Meeker's article convinced him that he was coming around to the same viewpoint. Vickers then prepared an article which appeared in the Denver Tribune entitled "Lo, the Poor Indian!" The substance of the article appeared in reprints entitled "The Utes Must Go!" Colorado opinion now seemed to crystallize and strengthen this slogan which served as the medium for action.

The article was read by Chiefs Douglas and Jack. They accused Meeker of writing it. He denied it but the Utes now mistrusted him and things from then on started to deteriorate at the Agency. The Utes had been very pleased when Meeker first came to the Agency and apparently straightened out the annuities situation, while food and supplies flowed in abundance to the Agency. They felt that he was capable of sending for the soldiers who would place them in chains and ship them off to the hated Indian Territory.

Although Meeker had a feeling that his influence with the Utes was waning, he nevertheless continued in his work to develop a model farm community at the Agency. An eighty-acre field was plowed and fenced. He was given permission by Secretary Schurz to order a threshing machine, a gristmill, and two wrought-iron plows.

Meeker had a house built for Johnson and the chief moved in with his wife Susan along with several of his other wives. Meeker also persuaded Jack to take up farming by promising him a new wagon. Jack's farm was located near the mouth of Coal Creek. Jack and his assistant Sowerwick, set up their village in this area. The village consisted of ninety lodges.

In spite of Meeker's best efforts, he could count on only Johnson, who apparently accepted the white man's way of life. Josie's efforts at enrolling the Ute children in her school finally ended up with only one student - Freddie, the young son of Chief Douglas. During this time however, Meeker had been able to pay off most of his indebtedness to the Greeley estate.

Another problem now confronted Meeker. There had been very little rain during the spring and early summer months. By July of 1879, fires seemed to blaze in dozens of places. Smoke could be seen for miles and miles. Normally these fires would be attributed to lightning or perhaps careless campers and hikers. Ranchers quite often destroyed sagebrush by fires. The Indians also fired certain areas in order to drive game out into the open.

With all of the sentiment against the Utes, the fires were now also blamed against them. The clamor against the Utes for setting the fires resulted in the Indian Bureau sending a wire to Agent Meeker. He was asked to see that the Utes, who had left the White River Agency to hunt during the summer, would be returned to the Agency. If military assistance was needed, Meeker was to call upon the nearest military post for aid.

Meeker was quite disturbed by this message. He had reported the absence of the Utes from the White River Agency to Major Thornburgh at Fort Steele. Although he had done this a number of times, no action seemed to be forthcoming. He had asked specifically that Jack's band and the Douglas band be removed from the Bear and Little Snake River Valleys. Governor Pitkin had sent a message to the Indian Bureau asking that soldiers be sent and that the Utes be moved to the Indian Territory.

Pitkin's message came to the attention of Douglas and Jack. They reacted by stopping all work on the Agency projects. They held meetings at the Douglas village as well as at Jack's farm. One can well imagine that the Utes were now literally on the "warpath."

It was at this point in time that Meeker may have had his first premonition of danger - not only to himself and family, but to the entire Agency personnel. His fears grew and on July 29, he made a trip to Denver to visit his friend, General Pope. He intended asking Pope to bring soldiers to the Agency.

In Denver, Meeker recounted the events that had occurred at the Agency and told General Pope that he feared an uprising by the Utes. Meeker concluded his remarks by stating that he was ready to resign after fifteen months of trying to change the Utes from hunters into farmers.

After listening to Meeker's account of the situation at the Agency, Pope advised him to remain at the Angency. Meeker learned that Pope had sent Captain Dodge and his company to Middle Park to investigate the fires. Dodge's camp would be only 176 miles away from the Agency and, in case of serious trouble, could come to th Agency at once. Pope felt that the nearby presence of the soldiers would keep the Indians in check. Dodge's company consisted of forty-four Negro Cavalrymen but Meeker felt that at least a hundred soldiers would be needed in case of trouble.

Although he was not entirely reassured by Pope's apparent confidence that in case of trouble, Dodge's troops could handle the situation, Meeker began his trip back to the Agency on August 5th. At Cheyenne, he took the Union Pacific for Rawlins. While on the train he met Major Thornburgh, the commander at Fort Steele. He asked Meeker if the Utes were still hunting and roaming away from the Reservation. Meeker replied that they were and also told the Major that his letters to him had been ignored, resulting in the Utes roaming in the Little Snake and Bear Valleys. This resulted in Meeker's farm program being a failure, since the Utes would not stay at home and work.

Meeker implied that it was the Major's fault since he had been asked several times to round up these Indians and return them to the Reservation, but had not responded. Thornburgh very patiently explained to Meeker that while the messages had been received by him, the request for soldiers had to be sent to his immediate superior, General Crook in Omaha. General Crook then had to forward the request to General Sheridan in Chicago and finally to the overall commander, General Sherman in Washington. No orders had been received by Thornburgh and without these orders he could not comply with Meeker's request for military aid.

Thornburgh informed Meeker that he had been asked to investigate the fires - supposedly set by the Indians. He had talked to many Wyoming settlers but they said that Jack's band, although hunting in the area, had set no fires. Meeker didn't seem to be impressed by the report and stated that the fires were in an area several hundred miles south of the North Platte Country.

The conversation between Thornburgh and Meeker ended on a sour note when the latter delivered a vicious monologue about the soldiers teaching the Indians bad habits and mentioned the murder of Indian women and children by the soldiers at Sand Creek and the Washita Battle.

Meeker continued his trip to Rawlins where he was met by Harry Dresser who was to drive him to the Agency. They were accompanied by George Eaton, a new employee who had been hired by Meeker, in his stopover at Greeley. As they were traveling along late in the afternoon, their wagon overturned and Meeker was caught underneath. His left arm was badly injured and the wagon was a total wreck. Dresser continued to the Agency and returned with another wagon. Meeker suffered great pain as he waited through the night for the arrival of another wagon.

All of these incidents failed to discourage Meeker. He came to the conclusion that he had been too good to his charges. His love had turned to hatred and he now considered them as cowardly and dishonest. He would teach them a lesson which they would understand. The use of force - soldiers, guns, and even chains, would convince the Indians that Meeker meant business.

As the month of August rolled by, Meeker busied himself with reading. He enjoyed reading a book on the adventures of Samuel Pepys. Meeker's whole personality seemed to undergo a change. He now became very distant towards his employes and moody. He even took Josie to task for watching the Utes race their ponies. When he discovered that Chief Jack had gone to Denver to complain about Meeker to Governor Pitkin, he told Jack he deserved hanging for his disloyalty.

The hundreds of Indian ponies that grazed in Powell Valley were really Meeker's biggest problem. They required acres of grazing area - an area that could otherwise be plowed up and put to good agricultural use. As a result, Meeker gave Shadrach Price orders to begin plowing up a 200 acre field which was to be put in winter wheat. This took place early in September, 1879. Since the area Meeker had selected to be plowed was a very rich pastureland, one can very well imagine how the Indians would react. Meeker meant it to be a test to determine whether the United States government would prevail or the Indians and their ponies.

No sooner had the plowing started then Jane and Antelope came to Meeker in protest. They argued that this particular tract belonged to Jane and the Agent had no right to have it plowed. The grass was needed for Jane's ponies to subsist.

The protest was ignored by Meeker and the plowing resumed. Several Indians, concealed behind sagebrush, fired their rifles in the direction of the ploughman, Shadrach Price. As the bullets whistled by his head he decided to stop plowing and not resume until the matter had been settled.

Now followed a week-long series of meetings at Meeker's office and also in Douglas's lodge. Sometimes the meetings were held in Jack's camp, further upriver. The situation had definitely reached a critical point. Some of the parents of the boys who were employed at the Agency wanted them to return home. They had heard disturbing reports from several ex-employes of the Agency. The boys didn't seem to be concerned, however. Fred Shepard wrote to his mother in Greeley and the following is an excerpt from the letter:

"As regards to my getting out of here soon, I have not felt as if I was in any danger so far as my life is concerned since I have been

Chief Douglas was in charge of the Utes who killed Agent Meeker and his employes at the White River Agency, on September 29, 1879.

Courtesy of National Anthropological Archives,

Smithsonian Institution

here any more than ever I did in your door-yard. I don't blame the Utes for not wanting this ground plowed up. It is a splendid place for ponies and there is far better farming land, and just as near, right west of this field, but it is covered with sagebrush----."

Meeker's next move was to write a letter to commissioner Hayt in Washington, which he did on September 8th. In this letter he gave a comprehensive report about the plowing incident. He stated that the incident was settled when Douglas and Jack agreed to the plowing provided Meeker would build Jane a house and corral, at another location.

Later in the day, Johnson came to the Agency office and asked to see Meeker. Mrs. Meeker informed him that her husband had just gone out. When Meeker returned, Johnson had already left. Meeker was still suffering from the accident that had injured his left arm. As he gingerly seated himself at his desk, Johnson returned and immediately started berating the agent. His angry words were overheard by Arvilla Meeker who later said that Johnson accused her husband of plowing up his land and writing lies about it to Washington.

Then Meeker further incensed the angry medicine man by saying that he had too many ponies and perhaps he should kill some of them. Upon this, Johnson lost all control of himself and seizing Meeker by the shoulders he literally pushed him across the room and outside, slamming the Agent up against a hitching rail. Arvilla's screams reached agency employees Fred Shepard and George Eaton who ran up and restrained Johnson.

Johnson then stalked away without uttering another word. The two employees helped Meeker back to his chair in the Agency office where he took stock of his condition. He was only bruised a bit but not seriously hurt. What bothered the Agent the most was that he had always considered Johnson a good friend and now he had turned against him.

The Agent spent a restless night. The next day he wrote letters to Governor Pitkin and Senator Teller. He also prepared a telegram for U.S. Commissioner Hayt. The telegram read as follows:

"I have been assaulted by a leading Chief, Johnson, forced out of my house and injured bodily, but was rescued by employees. It is now revealed that Johnson originated all the trouble stated in letter Sept. 8. His son shot at plowman, and opposition to plowing is wide. Plowing stops: Life of self, family, and employees not safe: Want protection immediately: Have asked Governor Pitkin to confer with General Pope."

N.C. Meeker, Indian Agent.

Meeker's mind was in a turmoil. He had come to the Agency resolved to win over the Utes by kindness and love but he knew now that if he sent the letters and telegram, he was committed to a program of force, brought on by hate. The letters and telegram remained on his desk until September 10.

On the afternoon of this date, the Agent received a visit from John W. Steele, from Rawlins. He owned the Rawlins-White River mail contract. He was unhappy because he had been losing money on this route due to the Ute trouble. He felt that it was the government's duty to protect his operation of the mail route.

When Meeker told Steele about the letters and telegram he had prepared, and which awaited mailing, he was very happy. If soldiers were sent in answer to Meeker's request, Steele felt the entire problem would be solved. He would be happy to deliver Meeker's telegram and be off for Rawlins, early the next day. The telegram would be received in Washington within four days.

No one was able to sleep much that night, for the Indians kept up a noisy war dance in the streets, near the Agency buildings. Steele departed at dawn, carrying Meeker's letters and telegram. Meeker himself stayed in bed till very late. Perhaps he had a feeling of hopelessness and despair, brought on by an almost impossible situation that he now faced. He had literally burned his bridges behind him when he finally had asked that the U.S. troops be sent to the Agency.

Upon receipt of Meeker's telegram in Washington, Secretary of War McCrary and General of the Army Sherman, gave their approval to the request and sent instructions to General Sheridan in Chicago, to contact the nearest military commander (to the White River Agency), and send troops to the Agency. General Crook in Omaha, was in charge of the military area and he sent orders to Major Thornburgh at Fort Steele by way of a telegram, which read:

"You will move with a sufficient number of troops to White River Agency under special instructions." Major Thornburgh had finally been given the go-ahead sign. He lost no time in getting his troops ready for the trip to the White River Agency. Time was now of the essence since the lives of Meeker, his family, and the Agency employees depended on how quickly Thornburgh and his men could respond to the urgent call for help.

CHAPTER THREE

The White River Expedition

The expedition was ready to move out on September 23rd. The column consisted of 153 soldiers and 25 civilians. There were 150 horses and 220 mules. Joe Rankin had been hired as a scout for the expedition. He had worked for Meeker at the agency and knew the country well.

Camp had been set up on the outskirts of Rawlins and here the various units gathered in preparation for the coming trek to the White River Agency. As the column moved out, they were cheered by many of the citizens of Rawlins who had turned out to see the soldiers on their way. Common opinion seemed to be that the soldiers would take care of the Indians in a few days and be back within a short time.

Major Thornburgh's deputy commander was Captain John S. Payne, and the adjutant was Lieutenant Samuel A. Cherry. The surgeon assigned to the command was Dr. Robert. B. Grimes.

The column was strung out for several miles as it moved down the dusty road toward Bridger's Pass and beyond that, the Little Snake River. Autumn, in all of its colorful beauty was a sight to behold, and the soldiers gazed in admiration at the panoramic splendor which unfolded before their eyes.

Late in the afternoon of September 23rd, the column reached the Little Snake River valley and camped there that evening. It has been said that the Little Snake River is 75 feet wide and one foot deep, and its beautiful blue water served as a perfect balance to the many-colored trees and shrubs.

It was at this point that Charlie Lowry was hired to serve as an extra scout and courier for the command. He would be used to carry messages to Agent Meeker at the agency since he was a friend of the Utes and knew the area well.

On September 24th, the column had marched over the divide and traveled sixteen miles down Fortification Creek. It was decided to leave Lieutenant Price and his infantry company at this location, along with eight of the supply wagons. This would be the column's supply base, from which it would carry on its campaign to the White River Agency.

Since Major Thornburgh had not heard from Meeker for several days, he decided to send a dispatch to him. The dispatch was prepared on September 25th and given to Charlie Lowry to deliver to Agent Meeker at the White River Agency. The dispatch

Panoramic view of the Milk Creek valley. Major Thornburgh and his troops approached this area from the far left of photo and rode up this valley, heading for the White River Agency, some twenty-five miles away. Thornburgh was killed while riding through the wooded area in center of photo. Troops retreated to mesa area near far right in photo.

Photo by Author

read as follows:

September 25, 1879

Mr. Meeker, Indian Agent, White River Agency, Colo:

Sir: In obedience to instructions from the General of the Army, I am now en route to your agency, and expect to arrive there on the 29th instant, for the purpose of affording you any assistance in my power in regulating your affairs, and to make arrests at your suggestion, and to hold as prisoners such of your Indians as you desire until investigations are made by your department. I have heard nothing definite from your agency for ten days and do not know what state of affairs exists, whether the Indians will leave at my approach or show hostilities. I send this letter by Mr. Lowry, one of my guides, and desire you to communicate with me as soon as possible, giving me all the information in your power, in order that I may know what course I am to pursue. If practicable, meet me on the road the earliest moment.

Very respectfully, your obedient servant,

T.T. Thornburgh
Major 4th Infantry
Commanding Expedition.

Not having heard from Agent Meeker for ten days, Thornburgh had no idea what the situation was at the agency. He hoped that by the time Lowry had delivered the dispatch to Meeker, the column would be within about a day's march of the agency. With this in mind the column resumed its march on the morning of September 26th, arriving at the Bear River (Yampa) after a dusty march of some twenty miles. Here the column went into camp near the Thomas Iles' ranch.

From this spot, Thornburgh sent Lieutenant Cherry and scout Joe Rankin to Peck's Ranch and store, about two miles distant. They were to check out the mail arrivals from Rawlins and also to check on the whereabouts of any Indians in the area. Lieutenant Cherry brought back a report that Ute Jack, or Captain Jack as he was sometimes called, along with ten other Indians were near there and wanted to meet with Major Thornburgh. Upon receipt of this information, Thornburgh called his officers together and met with Captain Jack and the Indians accompanying him.

After a period of smoking, Captain Jack shook hands with all the officers and then asked them what their reason was for coming to the area. Captain Payne replied that they were traveling. Captain Jack kept asking, "What you marching for?" Major Thornburgh informed him that he had heard of the difficulties between the Utes and Mr. Meeker. The soldiers had come to straighten out any dif-

— 24 —

ficulties between the Utes and the agent.

Captain Jack then wanted to know where Thornburgh had gotten his information. He was told that the agent had given him the information himself. Jack then said that Meeker was a bad agent and listed all of his grievances against him. He also wanted to know how many soldiers were in the column. Thornburgh answered that there were three cavalry companies and one infantry company. Jack had served with General Cook as a scout and already knew how many men were in each of the companies without being told.

Thornburgh and Captain Jack then became embroiled in an angry exchange with the major telling Jack: "I started out here because of the things I have heard, and if it has to end in war, then so be it. I received a notice that the Indians have the agent besieged."

The argument between Captain Jack and Major Thornburgh continued for some times. Jack seemed to have an argument for every point that Thornburgh brought up, concerning why he had come to visit the agency. The argument was finally brought to a close by Thornburgh saying he was a friend of the Indians but in carrying out his orders there might be some Indians killed as well as some soldiers. Jack's advice was that Thornburgh, accompanied by five or six of his men, go to the agency to straighten things out. The balance of his column would stay in camp while negotiations were carried on.

After Jack and the Indians had gone, Thornburgh drafted a message to be sent to General Crook, by way of the telegraph. The message read as follows:

"Have met some Ute Chiefs here; they seem friendly and promise to go with me to the agency; say Utes don't understand why we have come. Have tried to explain satisfactorily — do not anticipate trouble."

T.T. Thornburgh, Major, 4th Infantry.

The expedition got underway again late next morning, on September 27th, and began the march toward Williams Fork — a distance of sixteen miles from the camp on Bear River. The difficult terrain made travel slow — the road being deeply rutted and very dusty. The column overtook a wagon-train under George Gordon. This train consisted of three wagons and was hauling a threshing-machine, to be delivered to the White River Agency. Dishes and other annuity goods were also carried for delivery to Mrs. Meeker and her daughter Josie.

During the day's travel, two riders caught up with the column

Close-up view of Thornburgh Battle monument, on low hill overlooking the bench area where the soldiers were besieged for seven days, entrenched behind their corralled wagons.

Photo by Author

and warned Thornburgh that the Indians had told them the soldiers were coming and they were going out to meet them and try to stop them from crossing over into their reservation. Thornburgh thanked them but stated that his orders were to go to the agency and that was what he intended doing.

Camp was made on the evening of September 27th and all necessary precautions taken since it was believed the Indians might stage an attack during the night. Later on in the evening, messengers arrived from the agency. Wilmer E. Eskridge, an employee of Mr. Meeker's, brought a dispatch from the agent for Thornburgh. He was accompanied by an agency interpreter and three other Utes: Colorow (Colorado), Tonwak, and Mus-an-ah-watch. There were also three other Utes in the party.

Colorow informed Thornburgh that he had come to speak for Captain Jack. He opened the conversation by asking where the soldiers came from. He was told, from Fort Steele, in Wyoming Territory. Colorow then asked, in a very surly manner, why the troops were coming to the Indian reservation. Thornburgh informed him that he was asked to investigate the Ute trouble at the White River Agency and try to resolve them. Colorow then made the same proposal that Captain Jack had made previously. He asked Thornburgh to halt the troops and proceed to the agency with four or five of his men.

Thornburgh then read the dispatch sent to him by Meeker and then asked Lieutenant Cherry to read it to the assembled group of officers as well as Utes. The dispatch read as follows:

White River Agency, Colo.
Sept. 27, 1879

To Major Thornburgh
   or Commander of U.S. Troops
      between Bear and White River, Colorado:
      Sir: Understanding that you are on your way hither with U.S. Troops, I send a messenger, Mr. Eskridge, and two Indians, Henry, (interpreter) and John Augisley, to inform you that the Indians are greatly excited, and wish you to stop at some convenient camping place. Then you and five soldiers of your command, come to the agency, where a talk and a better understanding can be had.

This I agree to, but I do not propose to order your movements, but it seems for the best. The Indians seem to consider the advance of the troops as a declaration of real war; in this I am laboring to

— 27 —

undeceive them, and at the same time convince them they cannot do whatever they please. The first object now is to allay apprehension.

Respectfully,
N.C. Meeker
Indian Agent

Thornburgh, pondering what course of action now to take, decided to leave the troops and proceed to the agency with four or five men, as had been suggested by Captain Jack and Colorow. He also wrote a dispatch which was to be delivered to Meeker at the agency. The dispatch read as follows:

Headquarters White River Expedition
Camp on Williams Fork
Sept. 27, 1879.

Mr. Meeker, U.S. Indian Agent, White River Agency:

Sir: Your letter of this date just received. I will move tomorrow with part of my command to Milk River or some good location for camp; or possibly may leave my entire command at this point and will come in, as desired, with five men and a guide. Mr. Eskridge will remain to guide me to the agency. I will reach your agency some time on the 29th instant.

Very respectfully, your obedient servant,
T.T. Thornburgh
Major, 4th Infantry, Com'd'g Expedition.

Thornburgh was still in doubt as to the proper move to make in the situation that now confronted him. He decided to call a meeting with his officers to discuss possible courses of action in the matter. There was a distinct threat of an Indian ambush, should Thornburgh advance with four or five of his men, as requested by the Indians. It might be more practical to move the column up to within striking distance of the agency in case of an emergency.

The column subsequently resumed its march late on Sunday morning, September 28th. The late start was due to the Major's expecting scout Lowry to return from the agency with a reply to his most recent dispatch. The delay also provided a much-needed rest for both soldiers and their horses. Camp was made on Deer Creek, a distance of about eleven miles from the previous night's camp on Williams Fork. From this point, it was still about thirty-five miles to the agency.

Thornburgh felt that there was no need to hurry, at this point in time. He had sent a dispatch outlining his projected actions and would await the return of scout Charlie Lowry, with Meeker's

Ridge held by the Ute Indians during the battle with the soldiers. Most of the cartridge cases found along the length of the ridge came from Henry rifles, which are powerful enough to reach the soldiers' entrenchment area located in the field, below lower range of hills in photo. (Author's metal detector shown in lower left.)

Photo by Author

reply. That evening, Thornburgh called his officers together again to discuss plans for the next few days — at least until they arrived at the agency. He also had second thoughts about keeping the command in camp while he and five men went on ahead to the agency, to meet with Meeker and the Indians.

Since Captain Payne was the deputy commander, Thornburgh asked his advice on the plan that had been submitted to Agent Meeker. Captain Payne replied that he did not agree with the plan but since Thornburgh had already submitted it, he might be compelled to carry it out.

Scout Joe Rankin was also asked if he had any suggestions about the situation. He replied that there was a three-mile stretch through Coal Creek Canyon which was a likely place for an Indian ambush, should the soldiers decide to march to the agency.

Captain Payne then suggested that instead of leaving the command at a designated point, it should march to Milk Creek and go into camp there. From this point the Major would leave with five men for the agency. Then, as soon as night settled in, the column would march through Coal Creek Canyon and be near the agency before the Indians knew what was happening.

After more discussion, Major Thornburgh decided to follow Captain Payne's plan. He asked Captain Payne to write a dispatch to that effect, which would then be sent to Mr. Meeker. The dispatch was read to the officers and then signed by Thornburgh. It read as follows:

Headquarters White River Expedition
Camp on Deer Creek
Sept. 28, 1879.

Mr. Meeker,
U.S. Indian agent, White River Agency, Colo:
Sir: I have, after due deliberation, decided to modify my plans, as communicated in my letter of the 27th inst., in the following particulars:

I shall move with my entire command to some convenient camp near and within striking distance of your agency, reaching such point during the 29th. I shall halt and encamp the troops and proceed to the agency with my guide and five soldiers, as communicated in my letter of the 27th inst. Then and there I will be ready to have a conference with you and the Indians, so that an understanding may be arrived at the my course of action determined.

I have carefully considered whether or not it would be advisable to leave my command at a point as distant as that desired by the Indians who were in my camp last night, and have reached the conclusion that under my orders, which require me to march this command to the agency, I am not at liberty to leave it at a point where it would not be available in case of trouble. You are authorized to say for me to the Indians that my course of conduct is entirely dependent upon them.

Our desire is to avoid trouble, and we have not come for war. I requested you in my letter of the 26th to meet me on the road before I reached the agency. I renew my request that you do so, and further desire that you bring such chiefs as may wish to accompany you.

I am, very respectfully, your obedient servant,

T.T. Thornburgh,

Major, 4th Infantry, Com'd'g Exepedition.

The dispatch was given to Mr. Eskridge for delivery to Mr. Meeker. Since he left on the evening of Sept. 28th, Major Thornburgh felt that he would wait until the evening of the 29th, before moving his command. This would allow time for the dispatch to reach Meeker and perhaps he would have some reaction to the plan.

Charles Lowry, courier and scout for the command, returned from the agency, on the evening of the 28th. He told Captain Payne that the Indians were going to fight.

He said that Meeker had threatened the Indians and told them they would be arrested and placed in chains and shipped to the dreaded Indian Territory. Because of Meeker's threats, the Indians were moving their squaws and chilren away from the agency area.

Lowry then added this prophetic comment:

"————————Father Meeker said he would leave, but they would not permit him to do so. I have no doubt but they have all been killed by now. We will catch hell tomorrow, and don't you forget it. We will get it in the canyon. The Indians told me that if the soldiers come on the reservation that they would attack them."

Thornburgh had determined on his course of action and now knew that there was no turning back. The die had been cast and tomorrow would be decided by the fates. Would the soldiers make it to the agency in time to rescue Mr. Meeker, his family, and his employees? A deeply troubled Thornburgh turned in for the night, knowing that his slumbers might be short and restless.

Wagon wheel hub found at Thornburgh Battle site, by George and Tom Le Deit. Hub was found at spot where soldiers were entrenched behind their wagons, above Milk Creek.

Photo by Author

CHAPTER FOUR

Confrontation at Milk Creek

Major Thornburgh's column resumed its march on September 29th. He hoped to reach Milk Creek where the horses and mules could be watered. Milk Creek was four miles from Coal Creek Canyon — the place where an Indian ambush might be expected. Lieutenant Cherry was placed in charge of an advance unit of ten men who were to stay a short distance in front of the column and keep a sharp lookout for Indians.

As the column neared Milk Creek, it met a wagon train which was on its way to the agency, carrying supplies from Rawlins. John Gordon, the owner of the ten-wagon train, was surprised to see the soldiers and asked why they were there. Major Thornburgh told him about the trouble at the agency and that he was going there to help resolve any problems with the Indians.

Gordon became very excited when he heard this and asked the Major's advice, regarding the course he should take in view of the Indian danger. Thornburgh advised him to park his wagon train at Milk Creek until the present crisis had been resolved. He felt that it would only be a matter of a few days.

The column then continued on its way and reached Milk Creek. As the soldiers descended into the valley, they noticed that the grass was burning along the bottom land. Fresh trails also indicated that a large body of Indians had stopped at the creek to water their ponies. The column came to a halt and the stock was watered. However, the water in the creek stood in pools and there was no running water. Since the water supply would not be adequate, it was decided to move ahead to Beaver Creek, about four miles distant. Major Thornburgh knew that this was risky business since the proposed camping site at Beaver Creek was well within the Indian reservation boundaries.

After the stock had been watered the march continued. Lieutenant Cherry was well in advance of the main column as it crossed Milk Creek and headed for Beaver Creek. It was now eleven o'clock in the morning. Suddenly, Lieutenant Cherry was observed, waving his hat wildly — a sure sign that the Indians were near. Captain Payne had his men dismount and deployed them in a skirmish line at the left of the trail. Captain Lawson, at Thornburgh's order, dismounted and deployed his company to the right of the trail.

Rock fort where Ute Indians were entrenched, on top of high hill overlooking the Thornburgh Battle site. Henry rifle cartridge cases were found in this area.

Photo by Author

Line of rock forts on crest of high hill overlooking the Thornburgh Battle site. Utes fired down at the soldiers who were barricaded behind their corralled wagon train.

Photo by Author

Lieutenant Cherry rode back to Major Thornburgh and reported that as many as 300 to 400 Indians were on the heights above Beaver Creek, ready to ambush the advancing column. Thornburgh gave orders for the men to stay dismounted and ready to fight. There was to be no shooting until the order was given.

Thornburgh then ordered Lieutenant Cherry to take fifteen men and move ahead for a reconnaissance and try to communicate with the Indians — if possible. Thornburgh thought that the Indians were merely staging a show of force to prevent him from going on to the agency and might still be willing to talk. Lieutenant Cherry was also reminded not to fire upon the Indians unless fired upon first.

Major Thornburgh and Captain Payne both tried to communicate with the Indians by waving at them. Some of the Indians responded by waving back. The Indians had selected an excellent position for the battle and they outnumbered the soldiers at least two or three to one. Thornburgh felt that he would have to concentrate his forces in order to stand a chance for survival. He therefore gave the order to fall back to the wagon train which was on a plateau, next to Milk Creek.

Lieutenant Cherry had carried out his orders (to advance with fifteen men) and as he was advancing, fifteen or twenty Indians also started out, apparently to head him off. When he came within about 150 yards of the Indians he took off his hat and waved it at them. The Indians responded by firing at him, wounding one of his men.

Cherry ordered his men to dismount and sent back word to Thornburgh that the Indians had fired at him. Captain Payne heard the firing and ordered his men to open fire on the Indians. Two of Payne's men were killed and a number of Indians were also killed. It was at this point that Major Thornburgh decided to have all of the units slowly fall back to the protection of the wagon train. He knew that he was outnumbered by the Indians and they also had the advantage in that they held the best positions as far as terrain was concerned. The wagon train would be the best defensive position from which to hold off the Indians until help would arrive.

The wagons were placed in a circle with the south side above the banks of Milk Creek. Through this opening the retreating troops could enter and barricade themselves within the circle of wagons. Major Thornburgh was riding back towards the wagon train. But when he was within 500 yards of his goal, a shot rang out and he toppled from his horse. An Indian marksman had killed the expedition's leader before he had a chance to really lead his men in-

Photo by Author

View of Thornburgh Battle site. The Indians held the hills in center of photo. The barley field in which the wagon train was corralled is just below these hills. Milk Creek runs below the enbankment at edge of field. Soldier's Ridge is shown running along bottom of photo.

to the battle.

The Indians were now pressing their attack, attempting to cut off the soldiers in their retreat towards the wagon train. Captain Payne as second in command, took charge as soon as he heard that Major Thornburgh had been killed. He directed the retreat as the soldiers slowly retired with Lieutenant Cherry covering the retreat.

A new problem now confronted the retreating troops. The constant firing had reduced the supply of ammunition to a dangerously low level. Lieutenant Cherry sent Sergeant Grimes to the wagon train to get more ammunition. He had to virtually run a gauntlet of Indian fire while doing so. His horse received several wounds but Grimes made the trip and returned with the ammunition without mishap. He was later rewarded with the Congressional Medal of Honor for this outstanding feat of bravery.

When Captain Payne reached the wagon train, he found that it was arranged with the long axis running from east to west, while the south side was being subjected to a fierce fire by the Indians who held the heights across Milk Creek. The corraled wagon train took in a space about 75 yards long and 25 yards wide. The entire command was finally within the confines of the wagon train and the animals were also placed within the corralled wagon train.

The Indians had possession of the high hills which were on the north and south of the wagon train and poured a relentless fire down upon the embattled troops and animals. Many of the horses and mules had already been killed or wounded. Their bodies were used for protection by the sharpshooters on the edge of the wagon perimeter. Three pits were dug in the center and these were used to shelter the wounded.

The soldiers then dismantled the wagon boxes, using bedding, corn and flour sacks to build up barricades within the circle. Entrenchments were made with pick and shovel. While the men were frantically working to construct these fortifications, the Indians kept up a steady fire — their Winchesters and Sharps rifles inflicting casualties on both men and animals. But the men would not be denied and the corral was finally in an excellent defensive condition.

The Indians had chosen an excellent position and had it not been for Lieutenant Cherry's discovery of their planned ambuscade, the entire column may have been destroyed.

Another new danger now presented itself. The Indians had set fire to the dry grass and sagebrush. A strong wind had come up and the fire was rapidly nearing the corralled wagon train. Heavy smoke enveloped the enclosure and the soldiers were hard put to defend themselves. The Indians seized upon this moment to mount a heavy attack but were kept back by the return fire of the desperate soldiers. The soldiers knew they had to stay in the enclosure because the Indians were waiting for them should they be forced by fire and smoke to evacuate their positions.

The men dug rifle pits, using whatever tools they could find. The pits were dug from eight to ten feet long, four feet deep, and four to five feet wide. The dirt was used to raise the outer wall defenses and also to cover the dead bodies.

Gordon's wagon train was parked within 75 yards of the soldiers' entrenchments. The fire set by the Indians reached the wagon train and, despite heroic efforts by Gordon and his men, was destroyed. The oxen had been released from the wagons and were either killed or driven off by the Indians.

The high tide of the Indian attack came and passed during the fire which threatened to destroy the wagon train and its occupants. The Indians were repulsed and the greatest danger had passed. The soldiers had met the challenge but at fearful casualties. At least six men were killed and ten wounded. At least three-fourths of the horses and mules were killed. Their bodies were used to bolster the barricades.

The Indians now moved in closer and used the ravines for cover. They were well-armed with the latest models of Winchesters, Sharps, Henrys, and Remingtons. Sometimes the Indians came within thirty or forty yards of the soldiers, but their fire was not too accurate because they dared not expose themselves too long to the return fire of the soldiers. By nightfall, the soldier casualties had risen to nine men killed and forty-three wounded. The Indians mounted one more charge and it came just at dusk. They charged to within forty yards of the corraled wagon train and then retreated with the loss of three or four warriors. This was the last serious attempt made by the Indians, although sporadic rifle fire continued until the column was finally relieved.

As evening set in, Captain Payne sat down with his officers and discussed the situation. They were all agreed that they could do nothing else but continue to fight until help came. The column that had marched out of Rawlins a few days earlier, amid an atmosphere of gayety and confidence, now sat soberly within its narrow confines, not knowing what would happen next.

As evening approached, smoke could be seen rising from the general area of the White River Agency. The officers reasoned that the Indians had probably set the agency buildings on fire and

View of Thornburgh Battle site, with monument in foreground. Milk Creek runs from right to left of photo, just below ridge in center. Thornburgh Mountain is in background.

Photo by Author

probably killed Agent Meeker and his employees.

The night of September 29th was a busy one for all the men. Dead animals were hauled off. A supply of water was secured from Milk Creek, the wounded were cared for, rifle pits were enlarged, and rations and ammunition issued.

Captain Payne decided to send four couriers to Rawlins, some 170 miles away, with news of the battle. Also, to send a telegraph to General Crook, asking for speedy reinforcements. He asked for volunteers and Corporals George Moquin and Edward F. Murphy offered their services. Scout Joe Rankin and John Gordon also volunteered to go on this dangerous mission.

Plans called for the four men to leave under cover of darkness by way of Milk Creek. Once clear of the camp, they were to split up and travel by separate routes — hoping that someone would reach the destination. At midnight, all was in readiness and each courier was given a copy of a dispatch prepared by Captain Payne. The dispatch read as follows:

> Milk River, Colorado
> September 29, 1879
> 8:30 P.M.

General George Cook:

This command composed of three companies of cavalry, was met a mile south of Milk Creek by several hundred Ute Indians who attacked and drove us to the wagon train with great loss. It becomes my painful duty to announce the death of Major Thornburgh, who fell in harness; the painful but not serious wounding of Lt. Paddock and Dr. Grimes, and killing of ten enlisted men and a wagon master, with the wounding of about twenty men and teamsters. I am corraled near water, with about three-fourths of my animals killed. After a desperate fight since 12 N we hold our position. I shall strengthen it during the night, and believe we can hold out until re-enforcements reach us, if they are hurried. Officers and men behaved with greatest gallantry. I am also slightly wounded in two places.

                Payne, Commander.

There was nothing to do now but wait, with the hope that at least one of the couriers would reach his destination. The Indians kept up a reduced fire which served to keep the men under cover. The earliest that help could possibly arrive would be within five days. Supplies would be conserved although there seemed to be enough to last for thirty days. All night long the men worked to

View of barley field area where Thornburgh's troops corralled their supply wagons and held off the Ute attack. (Author's metal detector may be seen in foreground.) Many cartridge cases and slugs were found here. Milk Creek is to the right of the field, where shrubbery is shown.

Photo by Author

View of ridge shown in foreground, held by Utes during battle. Many Henry cartridge cases were found here. Soldiers were besieged in barley field, in center of photo. The wagons were corralled in area of field, near the large trees in center of photo.

Photo by Author

strengthen their positions and by morning, they felt they would be able to hold out until the siege was lifted.

The command faced the next day, September 30th, with renewed confidence and hope. Although still pinned down by Indian fire they felt they were in a position to repulse any and all attacks. All day long the Indians kept up a steady fire. They killed all of the animals except fourteen mules. The soldiers wasted little ammunition and fired only when a good target presented itself. They day dragged by, with the suffering of the wounded and their pitiful groans further adding to the anxiety and concern of the soldiers.

The night of September 30 was comparatively quiet, but each night thereafter was pierced by rifle shots, noisy Indians holding their scalp dances, along with the mournful howling of coyotes. The Utes yelled insults at the soldiers which were returned in kind. The soldiers were able to get very little sleep due to the noise and clamor by the howling Utes. Each soldier hoped that tomorrow would bring an end to this unreal dream and that the Indians would be driven away by a relief column of U.S. Troops.

The morning of October 1st dawned with a slight chill in the air. Although there were still no visible signs of relief, the soldiers were confident they could hold out until help arrived. They were still under constant fire during the daylight hours, so water had to be secured and sagebrush gathered to make coffee and warm the beans — all this had to be done under cover of night.

As the day drew on, it became very warm. The smell of dead horses was almost unbearable — even though the soldiers tried to cover them with dirt. Evenings were cool and fires and blankets were needed to keep warm. The command had now been reduced to 90 able men, from its original roster of 153.

On the night of October 1st, as a water detail was trying to bring up water from Milk Creek, they were attacked by the Indians but the soldiers repulsed them and completed their mission. Enough water was secured for a twenty-four hour period. The wounded were attended by Dr. Grimes, who was himself wounded and in need of medical care. The Indians kept up a steady fire during the day and night, from their positions on the bluffs above the soldiers' camp. All of the horses had been killed and only twelve mules remained.

Although the soldiers were unaware of it, help was now on the way. Captain Francis Dodge in charge of Company D, 9th Cavalry (colored), had received orders to march to Captain Payne's relief. They reached a hill overlooking Milk Creek valley, on the morning of October 2nd, and saw the corraled wagon train, surrounded by

View of Milk Creek, which was the boundary line of the Ute Indian Reservation. When Thornburgh's troops crossed this stream, the Utes attacked them. They felt that this was a declaration of war on the part of the army.

Photo by Author

DEATH OF MAJOR THORNBURGH ... LE LEADING A CHARGE TO SECURE THE WAGON TRAIN.

Major Thornburgh was killed by a Ute Indian sniper's bullet at the beginning of the Milk Creek Battle. His men were in the process of retreating to the shelter of their wagon train.

Courtesy of National Anthropological Archives, Smithsonian Institution the Indians. Captain Dodge knew that his small command of 37 soldiers could not attack the Indians, but felt that his best plan would be to ride into the wagon train compound and join the soldiers there. He decided that it would be best to approach the compound slowly and carefully. The surprised Indians made no effort to stop him as he and his men rode toward Payne's command, amid the cheers of the beleagured soldiers.

Captain Payne and his men gave the new arrivals a rousing welcome. Captain Dodge wanted to make a charge on the Indians holding the bluffs to the north, but Captain Payne restrained him, saying, "I believe that would be foolish, Captain. By the time your troopers were mounted, they would have been exposed enough to enemy fire to kill or wound the entire company. Now that you are in the corral, it is best to keep under cover as much as possible. Pray like hell that help comes soon. As you have probably noticed, now that you have come in, there are a great many more Indians upon the rims watching our position."

Payne's words were prophetic, as the Indians kept up a steady fire for the next three days. The corraled wagons were located on a small plateau on the right bank of Milk Creek. Some hundred or more yards to the north was a long mountain at least 400 to 600 feet high, from which the Indians were able to cover every inch of the soldiers' entrenched positions. The cavalry carbines lacked the range of the Indian rifles. Had Payne's command been equipped with longer range rifles, it would have discouraged the Indians from coming as close as they did to the corraled wagon train positions.

October 2nd, the fourth day of the siege, greeted the troopers with a beautiful sunrise. After another night of fitful rest, the soldiers awoke, no doubt wondering whether help would arrive on this day or — perhaps the Indians would tire of the long siege and leave the area.

The fifth day of the siege passed without anything unusual happening. The Indians would try to approach the entrenchments by crawling up the Milk Creek bottom but never came any closer than about a hundred yards. The Indians were aware of the colored troops who had joined the soldiers several days earlier. The Utes kept calling to them, hoping they would expose themselves to the Indian fire. "Come out", they said, "you sons-of-bitches, and fight like men ————— Utes kill 'oor 'orse and mool, and kill oo."

Other insults were hurled at the soldiers in broken English and seemed to come from a white man who was with the Indians. When a horse or mule fell, the voice from the bluffs would yell, "Better go out and harness him again for your funeral." Or "Lift up your hats and give us a mark." Another comment, "Come out of your holes and fight square."

The Indians generally ceased most of their activities during the night, which allowed the soldiers to haul off some of the dead animals since the smell was nearly unbearable. A total of 148 horses and 106 mules were killed. Only five horses and two mules remained unscathed.

Sunday, October 5th, marked the seventh day of the siege. Supplies and ammunition were still sufficient, although the men were cautioned to fire only when good targets presented themselves. As dawn approached, a faint sound was heard by the embattled troops. Down through the valley came the welcome sound of "Officers Call". As trumpeter Inman responded with an answering call, the men rushed from their rifle pits, totally ignoring the Indians, and shouted with joy. The startled Indians now waited to see what the size of the new column would be. The wornout and exhausted men knew the siege was over and they would soon be going home.

The rescue column, led by Colonel Merritt, rode quietly into the valley and to the corraled wagon train. His men were received with rousing cheers and a hearty welcome. The tears flowed freely as these men, who had fought for their very lives, now realized that the long and painful ordeal was over.

Dr. James Kimball, who was a member of Merritt's column, now assisted Dr. Grimes in treating the wounded and getting them ready for the long trip back to their post.

The men and officers of Captain Payne's command had fought courageously and well during the long days and nights of the siege. They never gave up hope that help would arrive. Their trial by fire had ended and they had not been found wanting.

Ute Jack
a Vicious Ute - Killed by
a Shell

no. 110

Captain Jack, also called Ute Jack, was one of the Ute Chiefs who led the attack upon Major Thornburgh and his troops at the Milk Creek Battle.

Courtesy of National Anthropological Archives,

Smithsonian Institution

CHAPTER FIVE

The Massacre

About the time that Major Thornburgh and his command were leaving Rawlins to ride to Meeker's relief at the Agency, Meeker was busy with routine office matters at the Agency. On Monday, September 22, he sent a check to Horace Greeley's daughters — symbolically the last payment on his $1,000 debt. He had finally cleaned up a debt which had been responsible for his taking the job as Indian Agent. Perhaps now he could go home to Greeley and resume his duties there.

The fates conspired otherwise, however. On Tuesday, he had an argument with Jack, because he refused to issue annuity blankets to Jack's men before they left for the fall hunt in Wyoming. The next day he had another run-in with Jane, who berated him for not issuing rations to a Ute who was not a member of the White River bands.

The late September days were very warm while the nights were cool. An uneasy feeling seemed to hang over the Agency — a feeling of foreboding. On Saturday, September 27, Douglas came to Meeker, greatly perturbed. Meeker disclaimed any knowledge of soldiers in that area but said he would stop them at the reservation boundary, which was Milk Creek. He would also arrange for a meeting between the Ute Chiefs and the commander of the soldiers.

Events now seemed to move along with added momentum. In Douglas' village, the squaws took down their teepees and headed southward. On Saturday night, Charlie Lowry arrived with Thornburgh's message, sent from Fortification Creek. Meeker, now thoroughly alarmed, saw to it that the employees stood guard over the warehouse, which was filled with annuity goods. Meeker received another message from Major Thornburgh the next morning. This was the note that had been sent from the Williams Fork camp. The Major stated in the note that he would come in to the Agency, without soldiers. Meeker read the contents of the note to Jack, who seemed to be satisfied that the soldiers were not going to cross the boundary line of the reservation. He informed Meeker that his warriors had been stationed in Coal Creek Canyon, ready to ambush the soldiers if they crossed Milk Creek and headed through the canyon.

On Saturday and Sunday nights the Indians staged war dances, outside of the Agency buildings. Charlie Lowry, as well as the Agency employees, were kept awake most of the two-night revelry by the Indians. One of the Greeley boys, Frank Dresser, wrote his mother a letter in which he asked her not to be worried about his safety, writing: "We are as safe and sleep as soundly as if in your quiet town of Greeley." This false sense of security on the part of the employees contributed to their downfall later.

On Monday, September 29, there seemed to be more Utes hanging around the kitchen, begging for food. The Indian squaws had all left the Agency and the bucks were looking for food. Josie and Mrs. Price, assisted by Arvilla, then busied themselves with the morning chores. Meeker prepared a telegram to the Indian Bureau, which Harry Dresser was to take to the Western Union station at Rawlins. The telegram read as follows:

"Major Thornburgh, Fourth Infantry, leaves his command 50 miles distant and comes today with five men. Indians propose to fight if troops advance. A talk will be held tomorrow. Captain Dodge, 9th Cavalry is at Steamboat Springs with orders to break up Indian stores and keep Indians on Reservation. Sales of guns and ammunition brisk for ten days past. When Captain Dodge commences to enforce law, no living here without troops.

N.C. Meeker, Agent.

Shadrach Price, the man who had been doing the ploughing, loaded up his Winchester and left in the family quarters. He told his wife Ellen not to worry and that this was just a safety measure. Not long after, the three women who were working in the kitchen, saw an Indian riding frantically towards the tepee of Chief Douglas.

After the rider had conferred with Douglas, the chief hurried to the Agent's office. He told Meeker that he had just received news that the soldiers had arrived at Milk Creek and some of them had already crossed the Reservation boundary. Meeker replied that this could not be possible since the soldiers did not know the area and may have crossed the boundary by mistake.

While Douglas and Meeker were talking, Wilmer Eskridge came in with the message that Thornburgh had sent from Deer Creek. In this message, Thornburgh had stated he would come in to speak to the Agent and the Indians, accompanied by only five soldiers. When Meeker told Douglas the contents of the message, he seemed very happy, shaking Meeker's hand and then leaving to tell the news to the other Utes.

Meeker then sent the following note to Thornburgh, which would be delivered by Wilmer Eskridge. It read as follows:

Roadside sign near site of the original White River Indian Agency. Agency was located in narrow White River valley, a short distance behind this sign.

Photo by Author

MARKER NEAR RIVER IS SITE OF ORIGINAL
WHITE RIVER INDIAN AGENCY
ESTABLISHED BY THE TREATY OF 1868 TO
SERVE THE NORTHERN UTES. POST OFFICE
ESTABLISHED AS WHITE RIVER, SEPT. 29, 1871.
NAME CHANGED TO MEEKER, AUG. 23, 1980.

Major T.T. Thornburgh
White River Expedition, In The Field, Colorado
Dear Sir:

I expect to leave in the morning with Douglas and Serrick to meet you. Things are peaceful and Douglas flies the United States flag. If you have trouble getting through the canyon let me know. We have been on guard three nights and shall be tonight, not because we know there is danger but because there might be. I like your last programme. It is based on true military principles.

Most truly yours,

N.C. Meeker, Indian Agent.

After writing the note, Meeker sat down for lunch along with Sowerwick, one of Jack's sub-chiefs, and Eskridge and some of the employees. When Eskridge had finished lunch, he prepared to leave for Thornburgh's camp in order to deliver the Agent's note. He was to be accompanied by two Indians — Ebenezer and Antelope, who would serve as his guides.

Meeker then returned to his office to read in his favorite book by Samuel Pepys. Some of the employees went out to work on a new building. A smiling Douglas came into the kitchen to get some bread and butter. He patted Josie and also shook Arvilla's hand. Douglas then left to see William Post at the Agency storehouse.

Now the kitchen was clear except for the women who were cleaning up the dishes and visiting as they worked. Flora Ellen Price left the kitchen to get her three-year old daughter May, and was surprised to see Ebenezer — one of the Utes who supposedly left with Eskridge. Not far away she saw some of the employees working on the roof of a new building. Arthur Thompson was spreading dirt while Frank Dresser and Mrs. Price's husband Shadrach, tossed up the dirt to him. Beyond them, she saw Douglas and about a dozen Utes, some of them armed. Among them she recognized Persune, Johnson's son Tim, Pauwitz and Antelope. (Antelope was the other Ute who was to have accompanied Eskridge to act as guide for the trip to Milk Creek.) Ellen Price was quite disturbed to see them and knew that something was wrong.

For a short period of time, events seemed to be suspended — something like the quiet before the storm. The very air seemed to be in a state of suspension. And then it happened. The Utes raised their rifles and blazed away at the unarmed employees. Art Thompson, who was up on the roof of the new building, was shot and fell

Historical marker on spot where old White River Indian Agency was located. Meeker re-located the Agency some twelve miles downstream. Marker is on the Dan Seely ranch.

Photo by Author

Photo by Author

Historical sign about four miles west of Meeker. The White River Agency buildings were located in the field shown in background. Ute Indians burned the buildings and killed Meeker and ten agency employes. The site is located on the Aaron Woodward ranch.

Map of the Thornburgh Battlefield and the surrounding area. The battle began on September 29, 1879 and continued until Colonel Wesley Merritt lifted the siege on October 5, 1879.

THORNBURGH BATTLE AREA
ON MILK CREEK
SEPTEMBER 29, 1879

HIGH HILLS

▢ - (CORRALLED) WAGONS OF SOLDIERS

O - SOLDIER POSITIONS

X - INDIAN POSITIONS

(A) - SPOT WHERE THORNBURGH FELL

🏛 - THORNBURGH BATTLE MONUMENT

STEEP

LOW RIDGE X

LOW RIDGE X

MILK CREEK

← TO SQUIRE RANCH

DIRT ROAD TO YELLOW JACKET PASS

INDIAN RIDGE

— 56 —

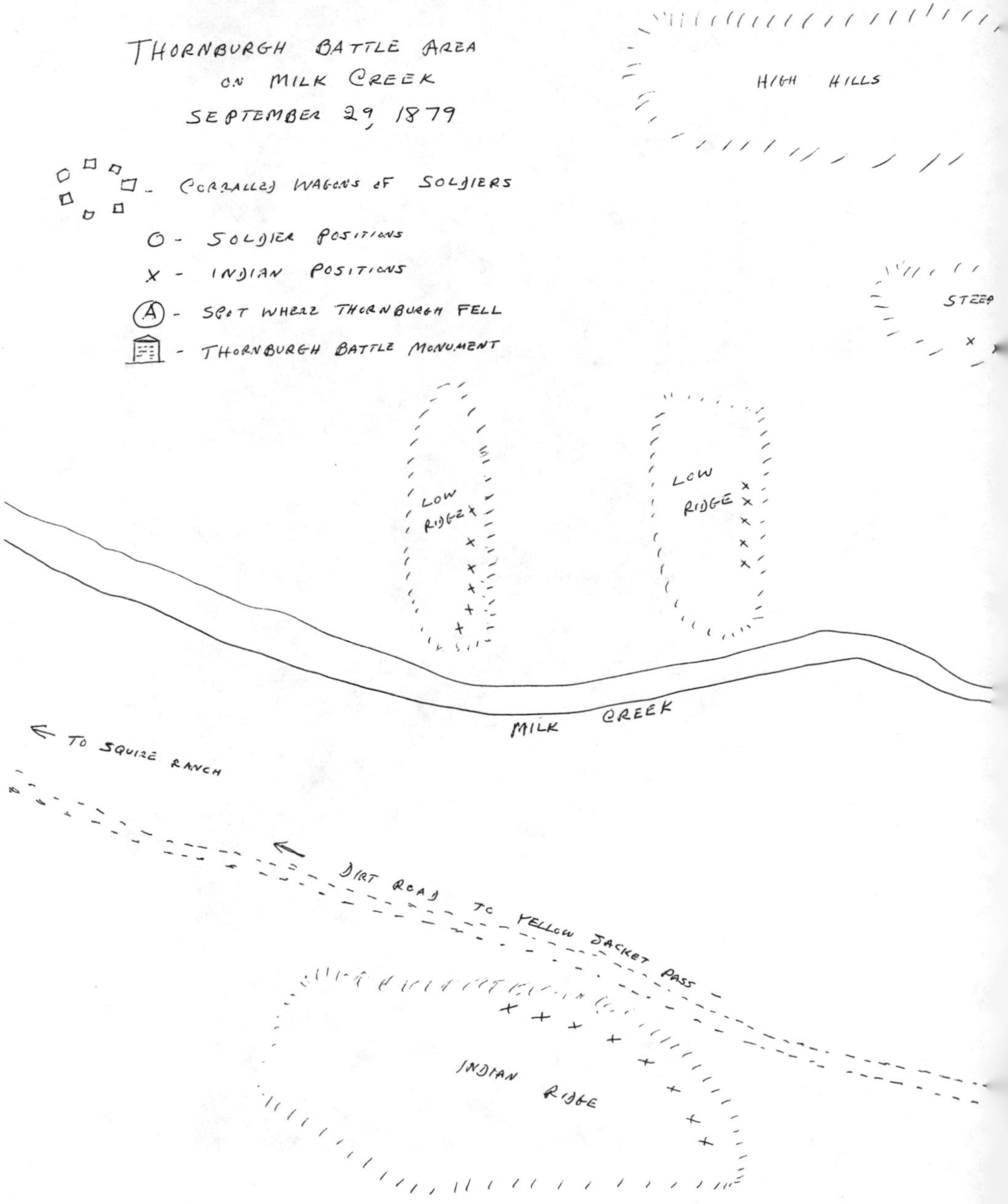

N

W E

S

THORNBURGH
MOUNTAIN

HIGH HILL
x x x x x x

LONG HILL

ET AREA

WAGON TRAIN

A

RIFLE
PITS

MILK CREEK

wood GROVE

TO WELLMAN RANCH

VALLEY AREA

MONUMENT

STEEP HILL

Indian ROCK FORTS

from the roof. Shadrach Price was shot in the abdomen, staggered and fell. Post was heard begging the Utes not to kill him. His pleas went unheeded. Frank Dresser ran to the boarding-house while Mrs. Price took her screaming daughter May and ran into her bedroom. Frank Dresser followed her into the bedroom and seeing the Winchester on the bureau where Shadrach had left it, seized it and fired at the Utes, killing Jata, Johnson's brother. Mrs. Price then took May and ran to Josie's bedroom, joining Josie, Arvilla, and her son Johnnie, under Josie's bed.

The Utes had fired the building and the smoke caused them to leave the building and run across the street to the adobe milkhouse. Frank Dresser helped them reach the milkhouse and then piled milk cans against the door. He had received a bullet wound in the leg, which Arvilla now dressed.

The milkhouse was of solid adobe construction and was used to store the milk from the Agency cows. It had only one small window and besides being damp, had very little air in it. They stayed there from about 2 P.M. until 6:00 p.m. As they sat there in stunned misbelief, they wondered what was happening to them and why. Mrs. Meeker began weeping and was very concerned as to what may have happened to her husband. He had worked so hard to better the lot of his Indian wards. Josie had grown to love these Indians and could only explain their acts by saying that there must be an outside influence that had created this situation — that had caused them to kill the people who were trying to help them. Mrs. Price was terrorized. Frank Dresser listened to the guns firing outside and could tell when an Agency gun was fired by its sound. The Indians had stolen the guns from the Agency, apparently just a short time before the massacre. Mrs. Price's children finally cried themselves to sleep.

As the terrified group huddled in the milkhouse, waiting for darkness to fall, they thought perhaps they could make a break for it and escape into the sagebrush beyond the agency buildings. Soon however, the milkhouse began to fill with smoke, making it difficult to breathe. They decided to make a run for it. They were running past the Agent's office and decided to go in. The room appeared to be undisturbed and on the desk lay a copy of the "Diary And Correspondence Of Samuel Pepys," just as Meeker had left it.

Finding that the room had not been disturbed by the Indians, Josie and the others thought that perhaps they could hide under the bed. They decided against it since they reasoned that the Indians would soon set the Agency office on fire also. Looking through the window of the office, they saw the Indians busily taking blankets

Photo of Powell Park area where Agency was located. Trees shown in center line the banks of the White River. Meeker and his employes were killed near the area shown in center — small rise in front of trees.

Photo by Author

Metal pole with metal ball on top is located at spot where Meeker fell. Outlines in grassed area in foreground mark remains of Agency buildings which were burned by the Indians. This land is in its original state, having never been plowed up.

Photo by Author

and other annuity goods from the burning buildings. Seeing that the Indians were all apparently occupied, they decided to make a dash for it across the plowed field and into the safety of the sagebrush beyond. The sagebrush was fairly high and might conceal them from the Indians allowing them to make their escape.

Frank Dresser told the others to keep in single file so that the buildings would shield them from the Indians and to run for their lives. They ran out of the Agency building and into the plowed field to the north of the Agency. Frank Dresser ran on ahead, while the others were slowed down by the little children and also Arvilla, who was lame.

They had covered about one hundred yards when a fiendish yell told them the Indians had discovered them. Frank Dresser shouted to the others, "Run! Run! Now or never!" He fired his rifle at the Indians but they continued coming, firing their rifles in return. Their bullets struck all around the fugitives as the Indians called upon them to stop.

Josie stated later that she didn't think the Indians intended killing them but shot only to frighten them and to get them to stop. Frank Dresser made it to the sagebrush but may have been wounded again. He had previously been shot in the thigh. Frank was without shoes, vest, or coat, and would find it difficult to travel through the cactus-covered country. He said he would try to reach Thornburgh's troops by that night.

Josie encouraged her mother to run faster but suddenly Arvilla was hit in her leg by one of the Indian bullets, but was not seriously injured. All the while the Indians kept shouting "Stop, Squaw! White Squaw, stop!" and "We no shoot! Come with us!"

Arvilla dropped to the ground and as she lay there, she saw the Indians capture Josie and Mrs. Price and her two children. Then the Indians came for her. One of them took charge of her and brought her to Douglas.

The Indians took their captives to the Agency, where some of the buildings were still burning. The Agency office had not yet been set on fire. It was now growing dark and somewhat chilly. Arvilla asked Douglas for a blanket and he sent an Indian to the burning building to get one. He returned with a hood, a shawl, and a blanket. She also put on a hat and picked up a number of other belongings. The Indians took the bedding and blankets. Later, during Arvilla's captivity, they refused to let her have one blanket to keep herself warm.

Arvilla then asked Douglas if she could get her medicine and her "Spirit Book." This book, so-called by the Indians was a copy

Photo of White River Agency buildings were located about 600 yards north (towards hills in background). Chief Douglas and Jane and husband lived in tepees close to the river.

Photo by Author

of Bunyan's "Pilgrim's Progress." She had administered to Douglas and his family members, when in medical need. Douglas allowed her to go into the burning buildings where she retrieved her copy of Pilgrim's Progress and medicine chest. Douglas had sent an Indian with her and because the chest was heavy, she asked the Indian to carry it. He refused to carry it and so the chest was left in the building.

As Arvilla went back to the Agency building, she saw a dead man lying on the ground. She walked up to the body to get a closer look. She was shocked to see that it was her husband. He was stretched out on the ground with his hands at his sides. Blood was running out from the corner of his mouth. He was naked except for a shirt, but the body had not been mutilated. Arvilla stooped to kiss her husband in a last goodbye. As she stooped to kiss Nathan, she saw an Indian looking directly at her and so she decided it would be best not to kiss her husband. Douglas later told Arvilla that her husband had been killed by a shot through the side of his head.

Arvilla said a silent prayer — saddened by her husband's death, yet relieved that now her beloved Nathan was free from worry and the agony he had suffered during his lifetime. She had loved him deeply and now wondered if she had sometimes been too demanding or harsh with him. His worries and problems were now at an end, while Arvilla faced an uncertain future in the hands of her Ute captors.

Josephine had been taken by a young Ute called Persune. Douglas tried to take her from him but after an angry exchange of words, Douglas walked away. Mrs. Price was taken by an Indian who claimed to be an Uncompahgre Ute. She was taken to Jack's camp which was about five miles from the Douglas camp. Arvilla was taken to the Douglas camp by several other Utes.

The captives were all taken to the Indian camp on the river. Some of the Indians were still occupied in stealing foods from the Agency. Most of the Agency buildings were now on fire. The Indians gathered up all the agency saddles as well as the horses and mules. There were loaded with all sorts of government goods — blankets, flour, cooking utensils, etc. Later on in the evening all of the Indians gathered at the river bank with their captives and loot and readied themselves for their retreat into the southern wilderness. They knew that the soldiers would soon come after them to punish them for their misdeeds. In the eyes of the Indians, however, they felt they were fully justified in doing what they did. When Major Thornburgh and his men crossed the reservation boundary at Milk Creek, that act as far as the Indians were concerned, amounted to a declaration of war. That is why they attacked the soldiers on Milk Creek.

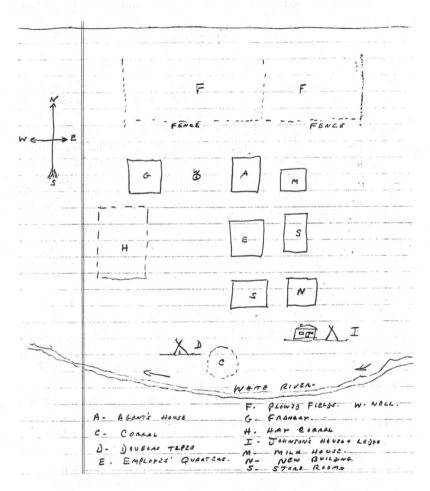

Sketch showing approximate location of buildings and facilities at the White River Indian Agency, in 1879. The Agency was located in the Powell Park area, about four miles west of present-day Meeker, Colorado.

Sketch by Author

Artist's version of the massacre of Nathan C. Meeker and his employes at the White River Ute Indian Agency.

Courtesy Colorado Historical Society

CHAPTER SIX

Captivity

Late on the evening of September 29, some twenty Utes with their captives, crossed the White River and started their trek southward. The path that they followed wound over a steep mountain and the travelers finally arrived at Jack's camp, which was five miles from the Agency. Camp was made and the captives were offered coffee, cold meat, and bread.

The Indians seemed to be in an excellent mood, talking and laughing as they told about the number of soldiers that had been killed at Milk Creek as well as the men they had killed at the Agency. Apparently nine men had been killed at the Agency. The tenth man, Frank Dresser, had escaped during the dash from the milkhouse to the safety of the sagebrush field.

While Josephine was with Persune, Douglas came along and held his cocked rifle at her head, threatening to shoot her. He did this four or five times but she held firm, telling him to shoot and that she was not afraid. Failing to frighten her, Douglas finally left, with the laughter of the other Indians following him.

The captives were then moved to the Douglas camp, about fifteen miles further on, heading toward the Grand River. Another incident took place, involving Douglas. He threatened Arvilla by placing a knife at her throat. She screamed and was heard by Josephine who called out in a loud voice:

"I'm safe, Mother! Don't be afraid of Douglas. He can't hurt you. He's only trying to scare you."

Apparently Douglas then desisted in his efforts to terrify Arvilla.

There were about twenty-five or thirty Indians who had taken part in the massacre, according to Josephine. They had plenty of guns and ammunition as well as whisky. She believed that the following Indians were actively involved in the massacre: Antelope, Warrsitz, Ebenezer, Persune, Johnny and Serio, who were Douglas's sons-in-law, Crepah, Tim Johnson, Charley Johnson, Charley, Cojoe, Powvitz, Thomas, Ahu-t-tu-pu-wit, Parintz, and Chief Douglas. Johnson may also have been involved, and his brother Tata was killed during the attack on the Agency by Frank Dresser.

Near midnight of the second day's march, the Indians stopped in a deep canyon. They were not sure of whether the soldiers were pursuing them, at this point. Travel was resumed until about two o'clock in the morning. A bright moon had made travel possible during the night and the weather was still fairly mild.

Some of the Indians were in favor of keeping their captives alive, reasoning that they could be used as hostages in case the soldiers overtook them. Others were in favor of putting them to death, by torture. In fact some of the Indians would strike the captives and threaten them in vile language and actions. Douglas was the worst of all and if allowed to have had his way would undoubtedly killed them all.

Camp was made, for the rest of the night, in a canyon. This was the Douglas camp and consisted of 80 lodges. This is where the squaws had traveled when they left the Agency a number of days before the massacre. This was also the place where Josephine was first outraged by Persune. She dared not refuse him since he was drunk and in a very ugly mood.

The next morning all of the men took their rifles and ammunition and prepared to leave the camp. They were going to fight the soldiers who were holed up at Milk Creek. Douglas also left with this group and was gone for five days. The captives wondered why the soldiers didn't come to rescue them. Little did they know that the soldiers were even now fighting to save their own lives.

From time to time some of the Indians would return, bringing back items of soldiers' clothing. They said they had killed some of them as they came out to get water from Milk Creek at night. The Indians seemed determined on killing every white man they met. They killed some of the freighters who were hauling supplies to the Agency. Supplies that were being hauled there for the benefit of the Indians.

The Indians told their captives that they had the soldiers surrounded in a hole or cellar. The Utes were on the hills surrounding the soldiers' camp and there was very little the soldiers could do about it, since they were greatly outnumbered. They dared not move out of their wagon train barricade during the daytime. Only at night did they venture forth to get water from Milk Creek. Even this was a dangerous venture since the Indians crept to within forty yards of camp in the cover of darkness.

Most of the Indian men who stayed in the camp were older men along with younger boys and squaws. The other men were out fighting the soldiers. Some of the squaws sympathized with the captives. One of them took Mrs. Price's baby, Johnny, into her arms and wept, saying she felt very sorry for the captives.

The Indian camp remained at this location until October 2, when it was moved some nineteen miles further away to a place on Rifle Creek.

Camp was made in a beautiful valley where the grass was plentiful and cool, fresh water was available from the stream that ran through the valley.

During this time, Josephine continued to be outraged by Persune, who had taken her as one of his squaws. Had he not done so, she would have been at the mercy of all the other bucks in camp. Persune told Josephine that within five days, the white men would come and release the captives. When she asked him why, he replied that Chief Ouray was very angry about the Utes fighting the soldiers. Many more soldiers would come and would overwhelm the Utes. Ouray was very upset because the Indians had killed Meeker and the others. Persune said he had heard that Ouray had sent an emissary to talk to the whites and try to arrange for a peace parley.

Councils were held by the Indians each night, including some warriors who had returned from the fighting on Milk Creek. Josephine was able to hear and understand some of the dialogue that went on at the councils. Apparently, the captives owed their lives to Susan, the sister of Chief Ouray and a squaw of Johnson. When most of the Utes in camp were clamoring for the captives to be burned at the stake, this courageous woman took on the opposition, refusing to be quiet. She told the warriors what the consequences would be if the captives were harmed and also how it would be of benefit to them if they were released. Since she carried a great deal of influence with Chief Ouray, the Indians finally decided that the captives would be spared.

On October 5, a Mr. Brady contacted the Utes at the camp. He had been sent by Chief Ouray with a message for the Utes to stop fighting the soldiers. The Indians apparently kept their captives hidden while Brady was in camp. In response to Ouray's order, the Utes stopped fighting at the Thornburgh battle area.

Soon Jack came into camp and gave a speech, followed by Johnson. They said that more soldiers were coming and this placed the camp in an uproar. The Indians were undecided on what to do next. Some wanted to move the camp while others were in favor of staying.

Josephine received a visit from Jack while he was in camp. He recited all of the things that the Agent had done which brought about the Massacre. He listed the following grievances: 1. The Agent had refused to give them a hundred pounds of flour when he asked for it, so he could go on a hunting trip. 2. The Agent would not issue blankets when he needed them - again, to leave on a hunting trip. 3. The Agent was always writing letters to Washington,

Josephine Meeker defying the Utes, who constantly threatened the captives with torture and death. Photo represents Chief Douglas aiming loaded rifle at Josephine.

and asking for soldiers to come to the Agency. 4. He blamed the Agent for stories in the Denver papers about the Utes setting fires and also getting the slogan started, "The Utes Must Go." 5. Accused the Agent of sending pictues of himself and family members to Major Thornburgh. These pictures showed the Agent and family shot and killed, supposedly by the Utes.

Jack also had a grievance against Major Thornburgh. He had gone to the major before the fight and asked him why he was coming to the reservation. The major had replied that he had come there to make the Utes behave and also to arrest a number to them for crimes committed. To be arrested were: Chinaman, Bennett, Johnson, Douglas, Jack, Colorow, and Washington. Jack futher stated that the major said he was going to arrest them, take them to Fort Steele and possibly hang them, if found guilty,

Among other things, Jack accused Major Thornburgh of starting the battle at Milk Creek. Apparently the soldiers carried plenty of liquor with them. They carried it on their persons as well as in their wagons. The Utes found two barrels of liquor on one of the captured wagons. The Utes apparently passed this liquor among themselves because those involved in the massacre were all drinking at the time.

Jack closed his monologue by saying that he had never wanted to fight the soldiers, blaming Douglas for the fighting.

The captives were treated like slaves by their captors. They had to bring water if an Indian wanted a drink. They had to get wood, and do any other chore upon command.

On October 7th, the camp was moved again. Most of the Utes who had fought at Milk River had now returned to the camp. Douglas said that many more soldiers were coming from Rawlins and the entire Indian camp was now afraid of what might happen to them.

As the camp was moved from time to time, the travel was through some of the burned areas. The Indians told the captives that they had set some of the fires in order to drive out the game. It would also provide a supply of fuel for the future.

On October 14, the Indians traveled for some distance. It was now quite a large camp since most of the warriors had returned. As they traveled along the column was stretched out for several miles. Camp was made near the Grand River, after a march of twenty miles through a very bad windstorm.

Camp was moved again on October 15, to a place near Parachute Creek. Some of the cattle from the agency had been driven along with the camp and this provided fresh meat each day.

Josephine was kept busy cooking and baking, during this time.

On October 17, a conference was held between Johnson and Douglas. Arvilla was now taken to Johnson's tepee. His wife Susan, cared very much for the captives and wept over them much of the time. She made shoes for Mrs. Price's children and was very good to them.

The Indians stayed in the camp on Grand River until October 18. High mountains surrounded the camp and the Indians would watch the progress of the soldiers from the heights, with binoculars they had taken from the soldiers. They could see for distances up to forty miles. They were apparently watching General Merritt's relief column which had raised the siege at Milk Creek and then continued towards the Agency.

The Indians told their captives that if the soldiers caught up with them they would ambush them, just as they had done at Milk Creek. They could hold the heights while the soldiers would be contained and killed in the canyon below. Although the Indians put on a great show of bravery, they would move the camp every time the soldiers came still closer.

On the morning of October 18, the Indians had planned sending twenty of their number to go back to the Agency area to watch for the soldiers. Before they could depart, some of the scouts reported that the soldiers had already passed the Agency and advanced about fifteen miles southward. The Indians panicked and the entire camp was a scene of noise and confusion. The squaws were busy, readying the camp for moving. The ponies were running around wildly and had to be rounded up and readied for moving the camp.

The Indians finally left their old camp around noon and covered a distance of about ten miles by the end of the day. Camp was made at Douglas' main camp on Grand River near Roan Creek. It was well suited for the camp, with plenty of grass, trees, and water.

Sunday, October 19, was a day the captives would long remember. All day long the Indians and their captives traveled along, with the rain coming down in torrents. By nightfall, a total to twenty-eight miles had been covered. The Indians became more and more excited as scouts came in periodically with news that the soldiers were drawing nearer. The captives were under the care and watch of three families. In case the soldiers came up and a fight developed, it was their job to keep the captives out of sight.

On that same night, Chief Colorow came into camp and met with the other chiefs. He advised them not to move any further south but to stop here. If the soldiers came, they would put up a

Chief Colorow, along with Captain Jack, led the attack on Thornburgh's troops at Milk Creek. Colorow was the lifelong foe of the white man.

Courtesy Colorado Historical Society

fight. Chief Ouray had told the White River Utes not to come to the Uncompahgre or Los Pinos Agencies. Since the Indians were nearing these Agencies, Colorow advised them to retreat no further.

The troops had been advancing steadily, but soon news arrived that their advance had been halted. The reason being that the Secretary of the Interior had sent a special agent, General Charles Adams to negotiate with the Indians for the release of the captives. When the captives heard the news they began to hope that their long ordeal would soon be over. They wondered however, if the Indians wouldn't continue to move them around and try to keep them hidden from General Adams and rescue team. Only time would tell and they prayed that a merciful God would release them from their savage captors.

CHAPTER SEVEN

Rescue

The entire country had been following the events that culminated in Meeker's death and the captivity of his wife, daughter, Mrs. Price and her two children. What would their fate be? Would they be tortured, outraged and finally killed — or would they be rescued from their Ute captors?

The wheels for their release were finally set in motion on October 13, when General Charles Adams received a telegram from Secretary Schurz in Washington, asking him to go to the Ute reservation and attempt the rescue of the women and children, held captive by the White River Utes. He would be acting in the capacity of an Interior Department special agent. Troop movements would be halted while the negotiations were in progress.

General Adams accepted and left at once for the Uncompahgre area to contact Chief Ouray. Although part of his trip would be by railway, there would be a stretch covering difficult mountain roads and old Indian trails. The weather was also now a factor since winter storms could set in at any time. Some 900 miles would have to be traveled on horseback.

Upon reaching Ouray's farm on the Uncompahgre, he was accorded a warm welcome by both Ouray and his wife Chipeta. Ouray related how depressed he had been when he received the news of what happened at the Agency and at Milk Creek. He was in poor health and had even considered committing suicide when he first received the news.

Adam's arrival revived some hope however that perhaps Douglas and Jack could be persuaded to release the women which might help allay the outcry of "The Utes Must Go." If the captives were to be released then perhaps the Indians responsible could be brought to trial and punished — not the entire Ute tribe as many whites were clamoring.

Adams and a party of five white men and thirteen Indians, left from Ouray's farm on October 19, heading downstream toward the Grand River. The thirteen Indians were led by Sapovanero, Ouray's brother-in-law. A buckboard was also taken along in which the women would be brought back — if and when released. Captain M.W. Cline was the driver. A supply wagon also accompanied the expedition and this was in charge of George Sherman and W.F. Saunders, who were also doubling as reporters for The Denver Tribune.

Photo showing Josephine Meeker and Flora Ellen Price, along with Johnnie and May Price, her·children. Josephine is wearing the suit she made while in captivity and which was made out of an annuity blanket.

Courtesy Greeley Municipal Museum

The Gunnison River was reached by evening and camp made near the picturesque Grand Mesa. Travel was resumed at dawn and a stop made near the Gunnison-Grand River junction, for supper. At this point, two messengers came into the camp with news from the camp of the captives. The soldiers were still marching south and the Indians, under Chief Jack, were very excited as they awaited the soldiers on Roan Plateau. The lives of the captives were now in great danger.

Upon receiving the news, Adams held a meeting with Sapovanero and they decided to keep on going during the night. They estimated that the enemy camp was about sixty miles distant. One of Ouray's war chiefs, Shavano, was a member of the Indian group that accompanied Adams. He volunteered the information that he knew of a deer trail that would save them at least twenty miles. It was such a rugged and steep trail however, that the supply wagon and buckboard would have to be left behind.

The group voted to take this trail in the interest of time and because of the great danger that now confronted the captives. Up and up the trail went, to a height of 10,500 feet. The weary men and animals plodded onwards — spurred on by the fact that the very lives of the captives now depended on whether or not the Indian camp could be reached in time.

The long night finally came to an end as dawn arrived. Shavano said that the Indians and their captives were encamped on a stream near Plateau Creek, only twelve miles farther. A breakfast of beans and coffee was enjoyed by the wearied men and then they continued onward. Suddenly, as they reached the top of a rise, the Indian camp was spotted, about a mile ahead, in a valley.

The Indian camp, composed of thirty-odd tepees, shone whitely in the morning sun. Ponies, goats, and sheep could be seen grazing in the meadow. Boys were hunting with their bows, for small game, while girls could be seen picking berries. Squaws could also be seen carrying wood to their tepees. No men seemed to be in sight.

One of the Indians with Adams, rode to Johnson's lodge and came back to report that Douglas and Sowerwick would be there soon, as they were expected to return from Douglas' Grand River camp. Adams rode toward the tents, accompanied by Cline. He rode towards the end of the line of tepees to Johnson's lodge. He continued to the last tepee and saw two squaws holding a blanket over the opening. Just then, a white woman pushed the squaw out of the doorway and came out of the tent. With her was a little white girl — Mrs. Price's daughter May! It was Josie Meeker. She was wearing a skirt and jacket which had been made up out of an annuity blanket. Adams notes that she was tanned and her blue eyes shone with happiness as she said: "I'm so glad to see you, Mr. Adams!"

Adams asked her how the others were and she replied, "Quite well, considering." He asked her if she knew that her father and the others had been killed, to which she replied: Yes. Asked if the Utes molested her and the other women, she replied — no. Adams seemed relieved but not quite convinced since he had heard many stories of how the Indians treated white women captives.

When Douglas and Sowerwick arrived, a very stormy meeting followed. The meeting was held in Douglas' lodge, which was quite large. On one side sat Adams and Sapovanero, while on the other side sat some thirty White River Utes. Douglas said the women would be released only after Adams had gone to the White River to halt the march of the soldiers (Merritt's column). Adams countered with the proposal that the captives must first be released, under Captain Cline's care, and then Adams would see that Merritt's march would come to a halt.

Hours passed by and there seemed to be no chance that an agreement could be reached. Finally Chief Sapovanero spoke, in the capacity of Chief Ouray's personal representative. Today was Tuesday, October 21. If the captives were not released and allowed to go safely to Ouray's farm by Friday, Ouray would personally lead his Uncompahgres to their camp, seize the captives, and force the White River Utes northward into Merritt's hands.

After Sapovanero's ultimatum, Douglas asked Adams if he had the power to stop the soldiers from their southward march. Adams replied that he represented President Hayes and that Merritt would follow his orders. A breakthrough had finally been achieved at 5 P.M. The women would be released and Adams would start for the trip to White River to meet with General Merritt.

As Adams finally left the conference tent, he saw Mrs. Meeker limping towards him. She had been hidden in the willows along the creek by Johnson. Josie was at her side and also Flora Ellen Price. Susan, the friendly squaw, came along behind them with Mrs. Price's two children — Johnnie and May. Mrs. Meeker appeared gaunt and pale, but not as bad as one would have imagined, after her three-week ordeal. Adams took her thin hand in his and told her the good news. She began to cry and thanked him for getting them released. "For myself," said she, "I don't care. Mr. Meeker is gone. I have nothing to live for. I am sixty-four years old, Mr.

Adams. An old lady, you might say."

General Adams then prepared a telegram which would be carried by messenger to Del Norte, from which it would be sent to Secretary Schurz. The telegram read as follows:

Camp On Plateau Creek
October 21, 1879.

C. Schurz
Secretary, Washington, D.C.

Arrived here this morning and have succeeded in persuading the Indians to release Mrs. Meeker, Miss Meeker, Mrs. Price and two children without condition, who will leave here tomorrow with sufficient escort. I go to White River to communicate with General Merritt. The Indians are anxious for peace and desire a full investigation of the trouble.

Charles Adams
Special agent.

For a short time, before Adams left to contact General Merritt, he visited with the three women and they gave him some of the highlights of their twenty-three day ordeal. Josie had been well-treated by Persune, who even offered to marry her. Mrs. Price had been offered three ponies for her young son, Johnnie. Arvilla had been mistreated more than the others. Douglas and his squaws had pulled every childish trick imaginable on her. He gave her a very hard horse to ride — without the benefit of a saddle. On one occasion he spit on her, threatened her with knives and said he would burn her copy of Pilgrim's Progress. In spite of all this, Arvilla administered to Douglas' baby when it fell sick and Douglas responded by giving her an extra blanket and pillow along with better treatment.

During their three weeks of captivity, the weather had been very mild with the exception of a hailstorm and windstorm. They were held in separate camps for the first two weeks but were then brought back together. Camp had been moved every time news was received about the soldiers moving closer to them. In all, camp was made in seven different locations. The Indians traveled from the Agency along the Hogback to East Piceance Creek, down Rifle Creek to the Grand River, and then down the Grand to Douglas' main camp on Roan Creek.

As promised, Adams left on the evening of October 21, and

with Sapovanero, headed north. They were accompanied by an escort under Sowerwick, and felt rather insecure until they reached Merritt's camp on Thursday evening. Colonel Merritt greeted them warmly and congratulated them on securing the release of the women and children. He had already received orders from General Sheridan to halt the advance of the troops until Adams could find the Indian camp and try to effect the rescue of the captives.

Adams prepared a telegram to Secretary Schurz which couriers would take to the Western Union station at Rawlins. He told about his meeting with Douglas and Jack and how they viewed the events that had happened — that the Milk Creek battle began when the soldiers crossed the reservation boundary; that Meeker and his employees were killed in reprisal for the twenty Utes killed at the Milk Creek battle; that those responsible for the Agency murders should be punished, but no others.

On October 25, Adams left General Merritt's camp and traveled to the Grand River camp of Douglas. After conferring with him, he continued on to the Los Pinos Agency, arriving there on October 29. Here he learned that the women and children had arrived safely at Ouray's home on the 24th. Meeker's son Ralph, was waiting there for them, to accompany them on the trip back to Greeley.

Ralph Meeker had been serving as a London Correspondent for the New York Herald, and heard of the White River Massacre on October 8th. He came back to New York and was named as a special agent of the Interior Department by Secretary Schurz. He then joined Inspector Pollock in Denver. The reunion of Ralph with his mother and sister was a tearful but happy one.

While at Ouray's farm, Inspector Pollock interviewed the late captives about their treatment by the Indians. The women denied having been outraged by the Indians, however.

They were taken by stage to Lake City, escorted by Captain Cline. Then on to Denver, arriving there on October 30. All along the way, at every depot in Walsenburg, Pueblo, Colorado Springs, and Denver, large crowds were awaiting them. All of the people seemed interested in seeing the women who had been held in captivity for twenty-three days and nights, by the Utes.

Upon their arrival in Denver, Arvilla, totally worn out by the long journey, went to bed at once. Josie and Flora Ellen Price remained in the lobby of Alvord House, with Ralph. They talked for hours with friends and well-wishers, while photos were being taken of them.

A tremendous throng awaited them as their train pulled into

This group photo includes Chief Ouray and his wife Chipeta. Both were good friends of the Meekers and welcomed Arvilla, Josephine, and Mrs. Price and children, after their release from captivity.

General Charles Adams, standing behind the Chief, was instrumental in obtaining the release of the captives.

Courtesy Colorado Historical Society

Greeley, the next afternoon. As Arvilla started to go down the steps, she was assisted by Max Clark. Also present were the A.E. Gipsons, David Boyd, and many other members of the original settlers of the Union Colony. Mary and Rozene, the Meeker daughters, were also there to greet them.

Literally thousands were on hand to welcome the Meeker women as well as Mrs. Price and her children. Arvilla wept as she looked west, up Locust Street and saw the fine homes and flourishing city which had been founded by her husband. She wept bitter tears in the realization that just when Meeker seemed to have accomplished some of his goals he was snatched away by an untimely death. It was always Meeker's plan to return to Greeley as soon as he had earned enough money at his agency job to pay for his debt to the Horace Greeley heirs.

They were taken up Walnut to Monroe and southward in Max Clark's carriage. Flora Ellen Price and her children stopped off at the home of one of her friends. Finally, the big, square Meeker house was reached — one of the finest homes in Greeley. As Arvilla limped into the parlor and looked around she noted that things looked very much the same as they had some sixteen months ago. A feeling of peace and security now was felt by Arvilla as she sat down in her old rocker. Perhaps now she could find some rest and quiet during the days ahead — days that would somehow never be the same because her beloved Nathan was gone.

CHAPTER EIGHT

The Captives Tell Their Story

Josephine Meeker, daughter of Nathan C. Meeker, gave a first-hand account of the events leading up to the massacre, her days in captivity with the Utes, and finally her rescue and release. The following account appeared in the New York Herald and was submitted by Josephine on October 29, at Alamosa, Colorado.

"The first I heard of any trouble with the Indians at my father's agency was the firing at Mr. Price while he was plowing. The Indians said that as soon as the land was plowed it would cease to be Ute's land. Two or more councils were held. The Indian woman Jane, wife of Pauvitts, caused the whole trouble. It was finally settled by the agent moving her corral, building her a house, putting up a stove and digging her a well. But Johnson, who was not at the council, was angry with the agent and the Indians when he found the plowing resumed. He assaulted father and forced him from the house.

Father wrote the government that if its policy was to be carried out he must have protection. The response was that the agent would be protected. Governor Pitkin wrote that troops had been sent, and we heard no more until summer came and all the Indians were greatly excited. They said that there were soldiers on Bear River, sixty miles north of the Agency. The next day the Indians held a council, and asked father to write to Thornburgh to send five officers to come and compromise and keep the soldiers off the reservation. The Agent sent a statement of the situation of the Indians and said Thornburgh should do as he thought best. The Indians who accompanied the courier returned Sunday to breakfast. A council was held at Douglas' camp, also at the Agency.

Meanwhile, the American flag was flying over Douglas' camp, yet all the women and tents were moved back and the Indians were greatly excited.

Monday noon Mr. Eskridge, who took the agent's message to Thornburgh, returned, saying that the troops were making day and night marches and it must be kept secret, but Thornburgh wanted it given out to the Indians that he would meet five Utes at Milk Creek, fifteen miles away from the Agency, on Monday night. He desired an immediate answer. Thornburgh expected to reach the agency Tuesday noon with the troops. The Indians, who at first were angry, brightened up and Douglas sent two Indians with one white man, Eskridge, to meet Thornburgh. But secretly the Utes were preparing for the massacre, for before Eskridge left with the Indians a runner was seen rushing up to Douglas with news of what I since learned was soldiers fighting.

Half an hour later twenty armed Indians came up to the agency from Douglas' camp and began firing. I was in the kitchen washing dishes. It was after dinner. I looked out of the window and saw the Utes shooting at the boys working on the new building. Mrs. Price was at the door washing clothes. She rushed in and took Johnny, the baby to fly from them. Just then Frank Dresser, an employee, staggered in, shot through the leg. I said, "Here, Frank, is Mr. Price's gun." It lay on the bed. He took it and just as we were fleeing out the door the windows were smashed in and half a dozen shots fired into the room. Frank Dresser fired and killed Johnson's brother. We ran into the milk room which had only one small window, locked the door and hid under a shelf. We heard firing for several hours. At intervals there was no shouting and no noise, but frequent firing. While waiting, Dresser said he had gone to the employees' room where all the guns were stored but found them stolen. In the interval of shooting Dresser would exclaim, 'There goes one of the government guns.' Their sound was quite different from the sound of the Indian guns. We stayed in the milk room until it began to fill with smoke. The sun was half an hour high. I took May Price, three years old, and we all ran to father's room. It was not disturbed. The papers and books were just as he left them. Pepy's Diary lay open on the table. We knew that the building would be burned and ran across Douglas Avenue for a field of sage brush beyond the plowed ground. The Utes were so busy stealing annuity goods that they did not at first see us. About thirty of them, loaded with blankets, were carrying them toward Douglas' camp near the river. We had gone one hundred yards, when the Utes saw us. They threw down the blankets and came running and firing. The bullets whizzed as thick as grasshoppers around us. I don't think it was their intention to kill us but to frighten us — but they tried to shoot Frank Dresser, who had about reached the sage brush. Mother was hit by a bullet which went through her clothing and made a flesh wound three inches long in her leg. As the Indians came nearer they shouted, "We no shoot; come to us." I had the little girl. The Indian Persune said for me to go with him.

He and another Ute seized me by the arms and started toward the river. An Uncompahgre Indian took Mrs. Price and her baby and mother was taken to Douglas' headquarters. We came to a wide irrigating canal which father persuaded the Indians to build. I said I would not cross it. The Indians answered by pushing me through the water. I had only moccasins on, and the mud and water were deep. The baby waded too, and both of us came out wet to the skin. As we were walking on, Chief Douglas came and pushed Persune away, and in great anger told him to give me up. I understood, some of the language. Persune refused to surrender me and hot words followed, and I feared the men would fight. For a moment I thought I would ask Douglas to take me, but both were drunk I kept silent and was afterward glad I did not go. Douglas finally went away and we walked toward the river. Before reaching the stream not more than two hundred yards away, both my conductors pulled out bottles and drank twice. No whisky was sold at the agency. Their bottles were not agency bottles. The Indian, Persune, took me to where his ponies were standing by the river and seated me on a pile of blankets while he went for more. Indians were on all sides. I could not escape. Persune packed his effects, all stolen from the agency, on a government mule, which was taller than a tall man. He had two mules. He stole them from the agency. It was now sundown. The packing was finished at dark and we started for the wilderness to the south. I rode a horse with a saddle but no bridle. The halter strap was so short that it dropped continually. The child was lashed behind me. Persune and his assistant rode each side of me, driving the pack mules ahead. About twenty other Indians were in the party.

Mother came later riding bareback, behind Douglas, both on one horse. She was sixty-four years old, feeble, not having recovered from a broken thigh caused by a fall two years ago. Chief Douglas gave her neither horse, saddle, nor blankets. We forded the river and on the other side Persune gave me his hat, full of water to drink. We trotted along until 9 o'clock, when we halted half an hour. All the Indians dismounted and blankets were spread on the ground and I laid down to rest with mother lying not far from me. Chief Douglas was considerably excited and made a speech to me with many gestures and great emphasis. He recited his grievances and explained why the massacre began. He said Thornburgh told the Indians that he was going to arrest the head chiefs, take them to Fort Steele and put them in the calaboose, and perhaps hurt them. He said my father had written all the letters to the Denver papers and circulated wild reports about what the Indians would do as set forth by the western press and that he was responsible for all the hostility against the Indians among the whites in the west. He said that the pictures of the agent and all his family, women and children had been found on Thornburgh's body just before the attack on the agency and the pictures were covered with blood and showed marks of knives on different parts of the bodies. The throats were cut and the agent had bullet holes in his head. I was represented by the pictures as shot through the breast, and Douglas said father had made these pictures, representing the prospective fate of his family and sent them to Washington to be used to influence the soldiers and hurry troops to fight the Indians.

This remarkable statement, strange as it may seem, was afterward told me by a dozen other different Indians, and the particulars were always the same. While Douglas was telling me this he stood in front of me with his gun and his anger was dreadful. Then he shouldered his gun and walked up and down before me in the moonlight, and said that the employees had kept guard at the agency for three nights before the massacre, and he mocked them and laughed at them, and said he was "a heap big soldier." He sang English songs which he had heard the boys sing in their rooms at the Agency. He sang the negro melody, "Swing Low Sweet Chariot" and asked me if I understood it. I told him I did, for he had the words and tune perfectly committed.

He said father had always been writing to Washington. He always saw him writing when he came to the agency. He said it was "write, write, write," all day. Then he swore a fearful oath in English. He said if the soldiers had not come and threatened the Indians with Fort Steele and the calaboose and threatened to kill all the other Indians at White River, the agent would not have been massacred. Then brave Chief Douglas, who had eaten at our table that very day, walked off a few feet and turned and placed his loaded gun to my forehead three times, and asked me if I was scared. He asked if I was going to run away. I told him that I was not afraid of him and should not run away.

When he found that his repeated threats could not frighten me, all the other Indians turned on him and laughed at him, and made so much fun of him that he sneaked off and went over to frighten my mother. I heard her cry. "Oh!" and I suppose she thought some terrible fate had befallen me. I shouted to her that I was not hurt, that she need not be afraid that they were only trying to scare her. The night was still and I heard no response. The Indians looked at each other. All hands took a drink around my bed then they saddled their horses and Persune led my horse to me, knelt down on his hands and knees for me to mount my horse from his back. He always did this, and when he was absent his wife did it. I saw Persune do the same gallant act for his squaw, but it was only once, and none of the other Indians did it at all.

We urged our horses forward and journeyed in the moonlight through the grand mountains, with the dusky Indians talking in low, weird tones among themselves. The little three-year-old, May Price, who was fastened behind me, cried a few times, for she was cold, and had had no supper and her mother was away in Jack's camp, but the child was generally quiet. It was after midnight when we made the second halt in a deep and sombre canyon, with tremendous mountains towering on every side. Mother was not allowed to come. Douglas kept her with him further down the canyon. Persune had plenty of blankets, which were stolen from the agency. He spread some for my bed and rolled up one for my pillow and told me to retire. Then the squaws came and laughed and grinned and gibbered in their grim way. We had reached Douglas' camp of the women who had been sent to the canyon previous to the massacre. Jack's camp where Mrs. Price was kept, was five or six miles away in another canyon. When I had laid down on my newly made bed, two squaws, one old and one young, came to the bed and sang and danced frantically and joyfully at my feet. The other Indians stood around, and when the women reached a certain point of their recital they all broke into laughter. Toward the end of their song my captor, Persune, gave each of them a newly stolen government blanket, which they took and went away. The strangeness and the novelty of my position kept me awake until morning, when I fell into a daze and did not open my eyes until the sun was shining over the mountains. The next day Persune went to fight the soldiers, and placed me in charge of his wife, with her three children. That same day mother came to see us with a little Indian boy. On Wednesday, the next day, Johnson went over to Jack's camp and brought back Mrs. Price and baby to live in his camp. He said he had made it all right with the other Utes. We did not do anything but be around the various camps and listen to the talk of the squaws whose husbands were away fighting the soldiers. On Wednesday and on other days one of the Sufanesixits' three squaws put her hand on my sholder and said 'Poor little girl, I feel so sorry for you have not your father, and you are away off with the Utes, so far from home.'' She cried all the time, and said her own little child had just died and her heart was sore. When Mrs. Price came into camp, another squaw took her baby Johnny into her arms and said in Ute she felt very sorry for the captives. Next day the squaws and the few Indians who were there packed up and moved the camp ten or twelve miles into an exceedingly beautiful valley with high mountains all around it. The grass was two feet high and the stream of pure, soft water ran through the valley. The water was so cold that I could hardly drink it. Every night the Indians, some of whom had come back from the soldiers held councils. Mr. Brady had just come up from the Uncompahgre Agency with a message from Chief Ouray for the Indians to stop fighting the soldiers. He had delivered the message and this is why so many of them had come back. On Sunday most of them were in camp. They said they had the soldiers hemmed in a canyon and were merely guarding them. Persune came back wearing a pair of blue soldier pantaloons with yellow stripes on the legs. He took them off and gave them to me for a pillow. His legs were well proportioned with leggings and he did not need them. I asked the Indians before Brady came where the soldiers were. They replied that they were still in 'that cellar' meaning the canyon, and the Indians were killing their ponies when they went for water in the night. They said, "Indians stay on the mountains and see white soldiers. White soldiers no see Indians. White soldiers not know how to fight!" One of their favorite amusements was to put on a negro soldier's cap, a short coat and blue pants and imitate the negroes in speech and walk. I could not help laughing because they were so accurate in their impersonations.

On Sunday they made a pile of sagebrush as large as a wash stand and put soldiers' clothes and a hat on the pile. They then danced a war dance and sang as they danced. They were in their best clothes with plumes and fur dancin' caps made of skunk skins and grizzly bear skins, with ornaments of eagle feathers. Two or three began the dance; others joined, until a ring as large as a house was formed. There were some squaws, and all had knives and pretended that they would burn the brush. The became almost insane with frenzy and excitement. The dance lasted from two o'clock until sundown. Then they took the coats and all went home. On Sunday night Jack came and made a big speech, and Johnson. They said more troops were coming, and ————. Brady had brought from Chief Ouray. They were in great commotion and did not know what to do. They talked all night and next morning they struck half their tents and then put them up again. Part were for going away, and part were for staying. Jack's men were all day coming into camp. They left on Tuesday for Grand River and we had a long ride. The cavalcade was fully two miles long. The wind blew a hurricane and the dust was so thick we could not see ten feet back in the line, and I could write my name on my face in the dust. Most of the Indians had no breakfast, and we traveled all day without dinner or water. Mother had neither saddle nor stirrups — merely a few thicknesses of canvas strapped on the horse's back, while the young chiefs pranced around on good saddles. She did not reach Grand River until after dark, and the ride, for an invalid and aged woman, was long and distressing. The camp that night was in the sagebrush.

On the morning of Wednesday we marched five miles down the river. A part of the agency herd was driven along with the procession and a beef was killed this day. As I was requested to cook most of the time and make the bread, I did not suffer from the filth of ordinary Indian fare. While at this camp, Persune absented himself three or four days and brought in three fine horses and a lot of lead which he made into bullets. Johnson also had a sack of powder. The chief amusement of the Indians was running bullets. No whites are admitted to the tent while the Utes sing their medicine songs over the sick, but I being considered one of the family was allowed to remain. When their children were sick they asked me to sing, which I did. The medicine man kneels close to the sufferer, with his back to the spectators, while he sings in a series of high-key grunts, gradually reaching a lower and more solemn tone. The family join and at intervals he howls so loudly that one can hear him a mile; then his voice dies away and only a gurgling sound is heard as if his throat were full of water. The child lies nearly stripped. The doctor presses his lips against the breast of the sufferer and repeats the gurgling sound. He sings a few minutes more and then all turn around and smoke and laugh and talk. Sometimes the ceremony is repeated all night. I assisted at two of these Medicine festivals. Mrs. Price's children became experts at singing Ute songs and sang to each other on the journey home. The sickbed ceremonies were very strange and weird and more interesting than anything I saw in all my captivity of twenty-three days.

We stayed on the Grand River until Saturday. The mountains were very high and the Indians were on the peaks with glasses watching the soldiers. They said they could look down on the site of the agency. Saturday morning the program was for twenty Utes to go back to the White River, scout around in the mountains and watch the soldiers, but just as they were about to depart there was a terrible commotion for some of the scouts on the mountains had discovered the troops ten or fifteen miles south of the agency, advancing towards our camp. The Indians ran in every direction. The horses became excited, and for a time hardly a pony could be approached. Johnson flies into a passion when there is danger. This time his horses kicked and confusion was supreme. Mr. Johnson seized a whip and laid over the shoulders of his youngest squaw named Couse. He pulled her hair and renewed the lash. Then he returned to assist his other wife pack, and the colts ran and kicked. While Mrs. Price and myself were watching the scene, a young buck came up with a gun and threatened to shoot us. We told him to shoot away. He said we were no good squaws because we did not scare. We did not move until noon. We traveled till nightfall and camped on the Grand River in a nice, grassy place, under the trees by the water. The next day was Sunday, and we moved twenty-five miles south, but mother and Mrs. Price did not come up for three or four days again. We camped on the Grand River under trees. Rain set in and continued two days and three nights. I did not suffer for I was in camp, but mother and Mrs. Price, who were kept on the road and got soaked each day. Johnson, who had Mrs. Price, went beyond us, and all the other Indians behind, camped with Johnson.

Friday Johnson talked with Douglas. He took mother to his tent. Johnson's oldest wife is a sister of Chief Ouray, and he was kinder than the others, while his wife cried over the captives, and made the children shoes. Cohoe beat his wife with a club and pulled her hair. I departed leaving her to pack up. He was an Uncompahgre Ute, and Ouray will not let him return to his band. The Indians said they would stay at this camp, and if the soldiers advanced, they would get them in a canyon and kill them all. They said that neither the soldiers nor the horses understood the country.

The Utes were now nearly to the Uncompahgre district and could not retreat much further. Colorow made a big speech and advised the Indians to go no further south. We were then removed one day's ride to Plateau Creek, a cattle stream running south out of Grand River. Eight miles more travel on two other days brought us to the camping ground where General Adams found us. It was near to Plateau creek, but high up and not far from the snowy range.

On Monday night an Uncompahgre Ute came and said that the next day General Adams, whom they called Washington, was coming after the captives. I felt very glad and told the Indians that I was ready to go. Next day about 11 o'clock, while I was sewing in Persune's tent, his boy about twelve came in, picked up a buffalo robe and wanted me to go to bed. I told him I was not sleepy. Then a squaw came and hung a blanket before the door and spread both hands to keep the blanket down so I could not push it away. I had looked over the top and saw Gen. Adams and party outside, on horses. The squaw's movements attracted their attention and they came up close. I pushed the squaw aside and walked out to meet them. They asked my name and dismounted, and said they had come to take us back. I showed them the tent where Mother and Mrs. Price were stopping and the General went down but they were not in for meanwhile Johnson had gone to where they were washing on Plateau creek and told them that a council was to be held and that they must not come till it was over. Dinner was sent to the ladies and they were ordered to stay there. About four o'clock, when the council ended, Gen. Adams ordered them to be brought to him, which was done, and once more we were together in the hands of friends.

Gen. Adams started at once for White River, and we went to Chief Johnson and stayed all night.

The next morning we left for Uncompahgre, in charge of Captain Cline and Mr. Sherman. The captain had served as a scout on the Potomac, and Mr. Sherman is chief clerk at Los Pinos Agency. To these gentlemen we were indebted for a safe and rapid journey to Chief Ouray's house on the Uncompahgre River, near Los Pinos. We rode on ponies for forty miles the first day, and reached Captain Cline's wagon on a small tributary of the Grand. Here we ————— two ranges of snowy mountains where the road was eleven thousand feet above the sea, brought us to the beautiful park of San Luis. We crossed the Rio Grande river at daylight for the last time, and a moment later the stage and its four horses dashed up a street and we stopped before a hotel with green blinds, and the driver shouted 'Alamosa!'

The moon was shining brightly and Mt. Blanca, the highest peak in Colorado, stood out grandly from the four great ranges that surrounded the park. Mother could hardly stand. She had to be lifted from the coach, but when she caught sight of the cars of the Rio Grande railroad, and when she saw the telegraph poles, her eyes brightened and she exclaimed, 'Now I feel safe'.

In closing this letter I want to thank Chief Ouray and his wife, and Gen. Adams. To them we owe our escape.

Josephine Meeker

Mrs. Meeker's Story

The following account was given by Mrs. Nathan C. Meeker, detailing events about the massacre and her captivity, and which account appeared in the New York Herald:

"I went with my daughter Josephine to the White River Agency, where we joined my late husband (the Agent) July 17, 1878. We

Photo by Author

Meeker Home, now a National Historical Site, was originally one of the finest homes in Greeley. Nathan Meeker felt that in building this pretentious home, he would convince the other settlers that Greeley was to be a permanent settlement. Mrs. Meeker and Josephine returned to this home after being released by the Ute Indians.

The sign in the photo reads:

MEEKER HOME

BUILT IN 1870

ORIGINAL ADOBE HOME OF
NATHAN C. MEEKER
FOUNDER OF GREELEY
AND UNION COLONY

NATIONAL HISTORICAL SITE

VISITORS WELCOME

did not like the site of the old Agency, as it was in a canyon. The altitude was too great for the practice of agriculture and the winds blew firecely and constantly. The government, therefore, gave permission to Mr. Meeker to move the agency twenty miles further down the White River to a beautiful valley, where the grass is always green, where there is no snow and where there is plenty of land to cultivate and timber in abundance. There was a magnificent view of the mountains and the rivers were swarming with speckled trout. I have not seen a more charming spot anywhere. Comfortable buildings were erected and fine avenues laid out. One of these, the main street, which ran as straight as a line from the canyon to the agency, was named after Chief Douglas. My husband was preparing to plant mountain evergreens on both sides of it. The agency grounds were well kept. The government Indian farm was enclosed with a neat wire fence, and it produced all kinds of crops. The Indians until the mutiny helped to cultivate the soil. They raised potatoes, beets, turnips, and other vegetables. The white employees sowed the wheat. In the agency yard I had some flowers, such as verbenas, mignonette, petunias, and others of a more common sort. The Indians seemed to like the improvements, and they admired the flowers. On ration days their children were to be seen with bunches of flowers in their hands. A large irrigating canal was built by the Indians under the agent's direction. It would water the whole valley. My husband discovered five or six good coal mines in the vicinity, at three of which there were large quantities of loose coal all ready for removal. It was as good coal as any in Colorado, and when used in the blacksmith forge it burned well.

Trouble began when the agent indicated an intention of plowing eighty acres of land lying between Douglas Avenue and the street. The Indians had not used the land except for their ponies to run on. It was open and undeveloped. As soon as he heard any dissatisfaction about the matter, the Agent called the Indians together and settled it by obtaining the consent of the main party of the initiative to plow. Chief Johnson failed to attend the council, and, when the Utes gave their permission he grew angry, and it was his son who shot at the plowman. Afterward Johnson said he was "No angry," but back of all this there were plans of wickedness and secret plotting ————— movements, increasing rumors, large sales of ammunition, and false charges that the agent had cut down the rations. This last was false. The government had reduced or changed the issue of rations for all the Indians. My husband gave the White River Indians regular and full government rations, but he had orders —————.

————— a succession of sharp explosions. It was startling and I knew what was coming. My daughter and I looked into each other's faces. Mrs. Price who was washing clothes at the door, rushed in, screaming, "what shall we do?"

Josephine said, "keep all together," and the girl was as cool as if she was receiving callers in a parlor.

The windows were shot in. Our first move was to get under the bed in Josephine's room to avoid the bullets, which were whining over our heads. Josephine had the key to the milk house and proposed to go there. The bullets were flying like hailstones, and we locked ourselves in the milk house, which had double walls filled in with adobe clay, and there was only one little window. We stayed there all the afternoon and heard no sounds but the crash of guns. We knew all the men were being killed and expected that the Indians would finish the day with the butchery of the women. Frank Dresser came in shot through the leg. He killed an Indian just as we let him into the milk house.

About five o'clock in the afternoon the firing ceased and all was still. Suddenly we heard the low crackling of flames and smelt smoke. Then we saw it coming through the cracks in the ceiling and knew that the destruction of the agency buildings had begun.

While in the building we barely whispered, and tried to keep Mrs. Price's babies still. As the fire was increasing, we left the milk house cautiously, and Josephine reconnoitered the enemy.

"It is a good time to escape," she said. "The Indians are busy stealing agency goods."

We went around in front of the agent's office, and found the doors open and things undisturbed except that some of my husband's clothing lay on the front stoop. We saw no one, living or dead, and no sign of anyone having been killed. We ran, in a line, with the buildings between us and the Indians, who were at the warehouse pulling out the goods, but we had not gone far before we were discovered, and the Indians made for us, firing as they ran. The bullets fell all around us, and one struck me on the thigh, ploughing through the flesh, just under the skin. It stung me like a wasp, and I thought it time to drop. I fell to the ground. The Indians captured Josephine and Mrs. Price first, as they were behind me, with Mrs. Price's babies.

You have my daughter's account of her experience. A chief, whose name I could never learn, came to me and said he was 'heap sorry'. He asked me if I could get up. I said "yes." He said he was "heap mad soldiers killed Indians," he saw them shoot and he was "heap mad." They would "no kill women and children." The Indians had so ordered it. He said that he would take me to Chief Douglas' house, and asked me if I had any whiskey. I said "No," and he asked if I had any money. I answered that there was some in my room in the building, then on fire. The Indian told me to get it and he would wait for me. He was afraid to go into the burning building. I got the money, the Indian urging me to hurry up, as he had a great way to go that night. We went to Douglas' camp, and the Indian made me count the money. There was $30.——. The—————————————————————————

I turned and saw Chief Douglas standing close by me, with the muzzle of his gun pointed directly at my face. I involuntarily cried out. Josephine heard me, and her voice came out of the night, saying:

"I am all right, mama, don't be afraid!"

Douglas lowered his gun, raised it again and took aim. I said nothing and he walked away. An Indian standing nearby said:

"Douglas no hurt you, he only playing soldier."

After resting for half an hour we remounted and rode until midnight, when we reached the Ute women's camp. Douglas ordered me roughly to get off the horse. I was so lame and in such pain that I told him I could not move. He took my hand and pulled me off, and I fell on the ground because I could not stand. An Indian and a squaw soon came and helped me up and led me to a tent. When I went to bed Douglas and his wife covered me with blankets, and I was more comfortable that night than at any other time during my captivity. Early next morning Douglas awoke me, saying:

"Runner just come; Indians killed heap soldiers; Douglas go to front; gone five days." He said I must stay in the tent and wait until he returned.

Douglas' squaw treated me very well for one or two days, then she began to abuse me and gave me nothing to eat for one day. While Douglas was gone his son-in-law told me frightful stories. He said the Indians "no shoot" me but would stab me to death with knives. One squaw went through the pantomime of roasting me alive — at least I so understood it. Josephine told me that it was only done to torment me. If Douglas had got killed I would probably have been punished. A row of knives was prepared with scabbards and placed in the tent for use. Then Douglas' son-in-law, Johnson, came to me and asked if I had seen the knives being fixed all day. I said "Yes." He replied that "Indians perhaps stab me and "no shoot" me. "You say Douglas your friend; we see Douglas when come back from the soldiers."

Many of the squaws looked very sorrowfully as if some great calamity were about to happen; others were not kind to me, and Freddie Douglas, the Chief's son, whom I had taken into my house at the agency and washed and taught and doctored and nursed and made healthy, came to me in my captivity and mocked me worse than all the rest. The Douglas blood was in him and he was bad. He said I was a bad squaw and an old white squaw. He tried to steal the old wildcat skin that I slept on, and stole my handkerchief, while I was asleep, and leered at me during my imprisonment.

Douglas returned from fighting the soldiers on Saturday night. On the next day his wife went back to the agency for the cabbages raised by the cultivation the Indians professed so much to despise. Douglas was morose and sullen and had little to say. He did not seem to be satisfied with the military situation but thought the Indians would annihilate the soldiers. Large numbers of head men and captains came to consult Douglas. They were in and out most of the night, making speeches and discussing things in general, as though the fate of the universe depended on their decisions. Douglas often asked me where the agent was. I said I did not know. Douglas rejoined that neither did he know. Mrs. Douglas treated me spitefully and her Chief was not much better, though he gave me enough to eat. When he was gone very little was cooked.

In a day or two Johnson became very cross, and early one morning we began to move again. It was a very long and terrible journey that I made that day. I rode a pony with neither a saddle or bridle nor stirrups. There was only a tent cloth strapped on the horse's back and an old halter to guide him with. It was the most distressing experience of my life. Not a single halt was made and my pain was so great that cold drops stood on my forehead. I could only cling to the pony by riding astride. We traveled rapidly over the mountains so steep that one would find difficulty in walking over them on foot. The dust was suffocating and I had neither water nor dinner. Josephine and Mrs. Price rode ahead. One of the mountains was so steep that after making part of the ascent Douglas' party had to turn back and go around it. This incident shows what hardship delicate women on bareback horses had to endure.

We reached a camping ground half an hour after dark and pitched our tents in the valley. The moon was small. I was so faint that I could not get off my horse nor move until a kind woman assisted me to the ground. I was too ill and exhausted to eat and went to bed without supper. We stayed at this place for several days. As the soldiers approached the Indians moved further south at intervals of two or three days until they reached the pleasant meadows of Plateau Creek, below Grand River, where General Adams found us. Before we reached this last place, Douglas permitted Josephine to come to see me every day, and the long hours were more endurable. The courage of the brave girl and her words of hope cheered me very much. My life would not have been safe had it not been for her influence with the Indians. She could speak some of their language, and she made them cease terrifying me with their horrible threats and indecent stories. She finally forced Douglas to give me a saddle, so that the last days of journeying I had something besides a bare back horse to ride again. It gave me great joy on one of the evenings of those terrible first days to hear her, as we passed each other in the moonlight, sing out cheerily,

"Keep up good courage, mother; I am all right. We shall not be killed."

The last evenings of our stay were devoted to songs and merrymaking by those who were not away on the mountains watching the soldiers. Mrs. Price joined in some of the choruses, because it helped us and made the Indians more lenient. They told a great variety of stories, and cracked jokes on each other and on the white men. They had dances and medicine festivals. Notwithstanding these hilarities, however, the Indians were troubled and anxious about the troops. Runners were constantly coming and going. The last rumor or —————.

Chief Douglas began to realize the peril of the situation. Colorow advised them to go no further south, though the troops were moving down from the north. Better fight and defend their camp, he said, then retreat. Chief Ouray, the friend of the whites, did not want the White River Utes on his domain. Douglas spoke of the agency as gone forever. He said it would have to be built again. The Indians had lost all, and with a sigh, he exclaimed:

"Douglas a heap poor man now."

When he had time he fell to abusing the agent, and said that if he had kept the troops away there would have been no war. One day I was told that a white man named Washington would come soon. At last an Uncompahgre Ute came from Chief Ouray and spoke very kindly to me, and as he sat by the fire said:

"Tomorrow five white men coming and some Indians."

Among them would be Chicago man Sherman, a great big peace man. General Adams, said they were going to have a talk and the captives would go home. The Uncompahgre said that a woman would be waiting at a certain place below the plateau.

Next day we were washing at the creek, when Chief Johnson

came and said that a big council was to be held and that we must not come up to the tents until the end of the meeting. Dinner was sent us by the squaws and we all began to have hopes of release, after being deluded with false predictions many times before. Finally we saw the foremost of the white men on the top of the hill by the tent.

When I first saw Gen. Adams I could not say a word, my emotion was so great. We had borne insults and threats of death, mockery and ridicule, and not one of us had shed a tear, but the sight of General Adams, Captain Cline, Mr. Sherman and their men was too much for me. My gratitude was greater than my speech. We owe much to the wife of Johnson. She is Ouray's sister and like him, she has a kind heart. Ouray had ordered us to be well treated and that we be allowed to go home.

The council was a stormy one. Various opinions prevailed. The war party wanted us to be held until peace should be made between the Indians and the government. They wanted to set us against the guilty murderers, so as to save them through us. After a few hours of violent speeches Mrs. Johnson burst into the lodge in a magnificent wrath and demanded that the captives be set free, war or no war. Her brother Ouray had so ordered, and she took the assembly by storm. She told the pathetic story of the captives and advised the Indians to do as Ouray requested and trust to the mercy of the government. Gen. Adams said he must have a decision at once or he would have to leave. That settled it, and we were set free.

Next morning, when we were about to start for the wagon, which was a day's journey to the south, Chief Johnson, who was slightly cool toward us, threw out a poor saddle for me to ride upon. His wife Susan caught sight of it and was furious. She flung it away and went to a pile of saddle and picked out the best one in the lot. She found a good blanket and gave both to me. Then she turned to her chief and poured out her contempt with such effect that he was glad to sneak away.

So long as I remember the tears which this good woman shed over the children, the words of sympathy which she gave, the kindness that she continually showed to us, I shall never cease to respect her to bless the goodness of her brother Ouray, the Spanish-speaking chief of the south. I trust all the good people will remember this.

November 12, 1879   Mrs. N.C. Meeker.

This flagpole has now been replaced with a tall, metal shaft with a metal ball on top. This monument marks the spot where Meeker was killed by the Indians.

Courtesy Colorado Historical Society

Mrs. Price's Story

The following is an account by Mrs. Price, relating her experiences during the twenty-three days of being held as a Ute captive. This account also appeared in the New York Herald:

"My name is Flora Ellen Price. I was born in Adams County, near Quincy, Illinois, and was married when I was twelve years old to Mr. Price. I was married in Wyoming and moved to Nevada, where I saw much of the Shoshone Indians. I went from Nevada to Girard, Kansas, and thence to Greeley with my husband, and thence to White River, where he was employed as a farmer at the agency. At first the Indians were very kind. They came to see us and their squaws would pick up my children and make much of them. With the exception of Johnson and two or three other Chiefs they didn't seem to be pleased with the agent. The trouble grew out of the plowing and the various improvements.

My husband said the agency employees told him that the agent was shot at by some young Indian there and the agent said so himself when they were talking it over in the room one evening. It was the general opinion, also, that he had been shot at by the Indians, but he did not want it to be known, on account of his family and because it would worry his wife. Besides, he was not entirely certain as to who fired and for what purpose.

The Indians were treated well as far as I know. The agency was kept in fine shape. Many improvements were made. A good table was set for the employees and they were only charged $3.10 a week, which is much less than is charged at the other agencies, where it is $4 and $6. The best provisions were bought and used and bought at Rawlins. Mr. Meeker refused to have any Indian blankets or Indian goods in the house so as to be free from all irregularities or charges of corruption. The Indians frequently ate at his private table, and the chiefs came and went as they pleased. They were treated kindly, but not allowed to take charge of the place, as they sometimes wanted to do.

The whole trouble, I think, was because the soldiers were coming in. They got very mad and on Saturday moved their tents across the river some distance and became uneasy and very anxious to know when the soldiers were coming in and if they were coming to the agency. I did not hear them make any threats against the agent. Douglas' boy shot himself accidentally in the foot, and Douglas remained at the river with several other Indians. They ran up American flags on Sunday morning. On that day the Indians were all around the place. There were a good many of Jack's band who seemed to be very friendly, but still they were frightened a little about the soldiers coming in, and on Sunday night all had a big war dance about a quarter of a mile from the agency. There were a good many present, including the principal Chiefs, headed by Douglas. Just before daylight on Monday morning Douglas got up and made a big speech to the Utes. The massacre followed on that day. Between the time of the dance and the time of the massacre I heard that Jack said he would meet the soldiers and get them in the canyon, where they would fight. Just before noon on Monday an Indian runner came in from where the Indians were on Milk Creek, and we supposed he brought news to Douglas, that they were fighting and perhaps had killed some Utes.

Douglas and several other Indians came in at dinner. Douglas was very familiar, laughing and joking in such a manner one would not have thought anything was the matter with him, though he had previously taken his little boy from the school and said he was afraid of the soldiers but that he would bring him back that evening. He picked around the table, was laughing and joking with Mrs. Meeker, Josephine and me. He drank a little coffee and ate some bread and butter. Suddenly he turned around and went outdoors. Mr. Price and Mr. Thompson and Frank Dresser were working on the building a few steps from the house. I saw him there when I went out after my little girl. Douglas seemed to be in very good spirits and was joking with the men. I had just returned and began washing some clothes when the Indians fired. I saw, I should judge — about twenty Utes around the house. The firing party was down at the barn, so Frank Dresser said. I saw the Ute, I did not know his name, fire at Mr. Price and Mr. Thompson and Frank. He was a White River Ute. I saw Mr. Thompson either running with the purpose to escape or because he was shot.

I rushed in, took my baby and ran to my room. Frank Dresser went to the boys' room where he found the Indians had stolen all their guns. He ran in after Mr. Price's gun and came out and shot through the window Chief Johnson's brother, who died two days afterward. We ran to Josephine's room. In a few minutes after twenty or thirty shots crashed through our two windows, and we crawled under the bed. The Indians were shooting all around. I could hear reports of guns in all directions and glass falling from windows. Josephine said the milk room is the safest place, and we ran there as quickly as possible, and reached the milk room just as Frank Dresser came in, and we all sat there quietly. My little boy was very nervous. May was quiet, and we remained there all the afternoon till nearly sundown and until they had set the buildings on fire. The shooting had ceased and we began to see smoke curling through the cracks. I said "Josie, we have got to get out of here; you take May, I'll take baby and we will try to escape in the sage brush across the road."

She took May's hand and went out, but first went to Mr. Meeker's room. It was not disturbed. The doors were open and the books were lying on the stand as he had left them. It was at first thought we had better secret ourselves in there, but I advised that we had better try to escape then, as the Indians were busily engaged in stealing the annuity goods. They had broken open the warehouse and were packing blankets on their ponies. We started for the garden when Frank said: "Perhaps we can hide in the sage brush and escape."

He ran through the gate in the field with Mr. Price's rifle. He was near the field when I last saw him, and I did not suppose he was hurt at all. Mrs. Meeker and I went into the field through the wire fence, and the Indians saw us and came toward us on the run, firing as they ran. Some were on foot and some were on horseback, and they said:

"Good squaw, come, squaw; no shoot squaw."

We then came out as it was of no use to run, and gave ourselves up.

I hesitated to go with them at first, and told them they would harm me or shoot me, but they said they would not harm us, and then came up and took my hands and pulled me through an irrigation ditch. Then they took me to the river as fast as they could, one on each side of me, to where the horses were, and then seated me on a pile of poles. I asked them if I could go back to the agency and get my money and clothes. They said no. I told them I was thirsty and a Ute who claimed to be an Uncompahgre — I don't know his name, caught me by the shoulder and led me down to Douglas' Spring, where he dipped up a pail of water and drank and then gave it to me. We then went back and the Indian packed his effects on a pony and spread a blanket on the saddle and told me to mount my horse. My baby was with me and May was with Josephine. She had taken the little girl from the first and carried my oldest child, May, all through our captivity. We were in three separate parties, but all in one company, not very far apart, through the different journeys. I mounted the pony and the Indian took a seat behind me. I held the baby in front of me and saddled the animal. About eight or ten Indians were in the company. Jim Johnson, a White River Ute, rode out in the party with us. He did not say anything to me only that he was going to take me to the squaw camp and he said the Utes "no hurt" me. I think he had a little whisky in him.

The road over the large mountains was so steep it was all I could do to sit on the horse. By this time it was quite dark. The Indian that rode behind me pulled a watch out of his pocket and asked me if I recognized it. I told him I thought I did but could tell better in the morning. He took it from his neck and put the leather guard around my neck, and said it was my watch. I have worn the watch ever since. It was Mr. Post's and belonged to his father; it was a family relic. Mr. Post was chief clerk at the agency, and had been secretary of the Greeley colony and was well-known in Yonkers, N.Y. where for many years he was postmaster and town clerk. This Indian treated me tolerably well during the journey.

When we arrived at the camp that night a squaw came and took my little boy from the horse and cried over him like a child. I dismounted and sat down in Pursune's camp. I wasn't at all hungry, and when they offered me coffee, cold meat and bread, I could not eat. After awhile Pursune's squaw got over her weeping, when they talked and laughed. All I could understand was then they repeated the soldiers' names and counted the number of men they had killed at the agency. They said they had killed nine. At first they said they had killed ten but I told them different, as I thought that Frank had escaped. They asked me how many, and seemed to accept my statement as correct.

They spread out some blankets for me to lie on, but I could not sleep. The moon shone very bright and everything looked ghostly. In the morning I went to Pursune's tent and sat by the fire. I was cold for I had nothing to wear except a calico dress and shoes. I sat there weeping — I could not help it — with my little boy in my arms. The squaws came around and talked and looked at me and laughed and made fun of me. I didn't understand what they said, only occasionlly a word. After a time some of the men came and talked to the squaws and looked at me and laughed. The Uncompahgre Ute, in whose charge I seemed to be, went off after his horses, and said at noon he would be back. He came about half-past twelve and brought two horses with him and said he was going to fight the soldiers. He put on his saddle, tied two blankets behind, put on his cartridge box, containing a good many cartridges and rode off. He said he would send a squaw after me, and I should be moved from that camp and remain until he returned from fighting the soldiers. One of the squaws brought a blanket and gave it to me. I went along with her and they told me then to go to work and bake some biscuits. I told them to build a fire and bring water, and

I baked biscuits and made coffee and ate pretty heartily myself, the first I had eaten since I left the agency.

About an hour after supper an old squaw ordered me to go with her to another tent to sleep, so I went to Henry James' tent, where I sat down. They had no fire but soon made one and the squaws crowded around. Henry asked me a few questions. He said he felt very sorry for me. He said he told the Utes not to murder the people at the agency. He had been assisting the issuing clerk and acted as an interpreter. He said they were friendly and he liked them very much. He said the Utes told him he was nothing but a little boy for refusing to kill the white men at the agency, but when they called him a boy he said it was too much for him. He had no more to say after that. He asked if I was going to stay all night in his tent. I said the squaw had brought me over there to sleep. He said, "All right; you stay here all night." So his squaw made me a very nice bed about ten blankets. I went to bed and she tucked me in quite nicely. I slept well, got up, washed myself, combed my hair and felt pretty well. Henry's squaw cooked breakfast. She made bread and prepared some coffee and fried venison and there was another squaw who brought in some fried potatoes.

I ate breakfast with my little boy in my arms, and presently Chief Johnson came in, angry and troubled. He said gruffly: "Hello, woman!" and shook hands. He sat down and presently three more Utes came to Johnson. Johnson took out his pipe and they had a smoke around, and they talked about the soldiers and their big battle.

Henry said to me, "You go now with Johnson to see your little girl, who is with Josephine." So I mounted the horse behind Chief Johnson and rode about five miles when I came up to Douglas' camp. I first saw Mrs. Meeker, and I went up to her, shook hands and kissed her, and felt very badly for her. She said:

"Don't make any fuss."

Josephine and my little girl had been to a ————— to get a drink. We sat down and had a nice talk until the squaws came and said I must go to Johnson's tent and the little girl to Pursune's. Miss Josie went down to Johnson's tent, where they sat down. Mrs. Meeker ————— for us to sit on, and asked if I was hungry. I told them yes, and they went to work and cooked some dinner for me.

The next day we moved from that place to another camp. It was a very nice place, with grass two feet high, and a nice brook of clear, cold water flowing through it. The Indians had killed many soldiers and were prancing around in their coats and hats putting on airs and imitating soldiers and making fun of them while going through a burlesque drill, and making believe they were the greatest warriors in the West. They took a great fancy to my little child and wanted to keep him. They crept into the tent after him and when they found they could not steal him they offered three ponies for him. In the afternoon, about 2 o'clock, they cut a lot of sage brush piled it up and spread over it the clothes they had stolen from the soldiers. Four of the Indians began to dance around them and at intervals fell on their knees before them and thrust their knives into them and went through a mimic massacre of soldiers. Other Utes kept joining the party that was dancing until a ring was made as large as a good sized house. They would first run away then turn and dance back the other way, yelling and howling like frescoed devils. They had war suits, fur caps with eagle features and they looked strangely hideous. They wanted Miss Josie and me to dance with them. We told them we could not — "We no sabe dance."

That afternoon Mrs. Meeker came over and we had an old-fashioned talk. She told us her troubles. They had threatened to stab her with knives, she said. Charlie, Chief Douglas' son-in-law, soon came around in a very bad humor, and as he could speak good English we didn't dare to talk much after he appeared. Mrs. Meeker said she felt as though she might be killed any night; that they treated her very meanly. Josephine seemed to be down-hearted, though she was plucky. I tried to cheer her all I could. The Indians would not let us go alone any distance from the camp. They asked me if I had any money, and I told them I did not, as it was all burned. We asked them where the soldiers were, and they said they were down in the cellar, meaning the great canyon, where they had them hemmed in. They said the Indians would lay around on the mountains and kill the soldiers' horses. The soldiers would not appear at all in the daytime. At night they would all come out only to be shot at by the Indians. They threatened that if I attempted to run away they would shoot me. Johnson put a gun to my forehead and told me he would kill me. I said:

"Shoot away, I don't care if I die; shoot if you want to."

He laughed then and would say: "Brave squaw; good squaw; no scare."

They also said that Josephine would very soon die as she drank no coffee and ate very little. I told them that it was the same at the agency, that she ate little and drank no coffee. They talked it over among themselves and said no more about it. They made fun of Mrs. Meeker, and said maybe the Utes will kill her. I said to them: "No don't kill my mother, I heap like her." "All right," they would say, "Pretty good mother; pretty good mother." Coho pointed his gun at me and threatened to kill me a good many times.

The Indians held considerable conversations with each other in regard to the massacre and tried to get information from us. They told stories of how the fight occured and who was concerned in it. From all that I heard of their talk I think Antelope or Pursune shot the agent. Chief Johnson said he shot Thornburgh in the forehead three times with the pistol, and then got off his pony and went to him and pounded him in the head and smashed his skull in. Then took some of his clothes off, but I did not see any of them worn in camp. The Indians, Ebenezer, Douglas, Persune, Jim Johnson and Charley Johnson were at the agency massacre. Jack was not there. He was fighting the soldiers. Johnson's brother Jata, was killed by Frank Dresser. Washington was on the ground. They all had gone and helped to shoot. Josephine said she saw an Indian named ———— there. I did not see any of the bodies at the agency. I only heard the firing and saw the Indians firing toward the buildings where the men were working.

The Utes said they were going to kill all the soldiers and that the women would always live in the Ute's camp, excepting Mrs. Meeker. Douglas said she could go home by and by when she would perhaps see Frank Dresser, who the Indians thought had escaped. They made me do more drudgery than they did Josephine. They made her cook and me carry water. One day we left camp about three o'clock in the morning. We had breakfast, only Josephine and I had roasted some meat on the coals. In the morning we rode all day in the thick dust without any water. We reached Grand River about sundown where we camped in the sage brush. To the south the mountains were very high and the country was bleak and bare on the north. The Indians said they were going to take us to the agency. The next morning we went about five or six miles and camped in a grassy place where the horses could get enough to eat, and remained there two days. We were camped very near a large mountain.

Johnson had field glasses and all day with his field glasses he was watching the soldiers, and only came down to his supper. The Indians took turns watching during the night, and during the day they covered the hills and watched the soldiers through their glasses. Runners came in with foaming steeds constantly. At last news was received that the soldiers were on White River, moving south. At this Johnson was very angry. In the morning the ponies were uneasy, and they could not catch them. Johnson's young squaw did not get around to suit him, and he took a black snake whip, caught her by the hair and gave her a severe whipping. She cried and screamed. He then went to help his other squaw, Chief Ouray's sister, pack up. They put us on one horse and strapped my little girl in a blanket behind Josephine. I had my baby in front of me. Johnson was very mad and pointed his gun at each one of us. I told him to shoot me in the forehead. He said: "No good squaw; no scare."

We started for another camping place south of the Grand River.

At last, one evening, we heard the white men were coming from the Uncompahgre Agency of Chief Ouray, to treat for our release. The next day the men came and I told Johnson's wife that we wanted to wash some clothes. She gave me some matches and a couple of kettles, and I went down to the creek to wash. While I was there Jim Johnson came with a couple of shirts for me to cleanse. He then went away, but soon came back again and said to me:

"Don't you come to the camp, for we are going to have a big talk with all the Utes. Don't come until Coos comes down after you."

Coos is his young squaw. Mrs. Meeker and I remained there in the brush all day, and dinner was sent to me by the squaws. Mrs. Meeker felt very much revived. You would not have thought she was the same woman. Captain Cline saw me in the brush and I held up my hands. He seemed to be looking at me but presently he turned away as if the Indians were watching him. He did not let the Indians know he saw me. Presently a Ute came down and said to Mrs. Meeker, "Come, Mother, white man saw." So I took the clothes which I had just washed and we walked carefully to the tent. There we met General Adams, Captain Cline, Mr. Sherman, the Los Pinos agency clerk and their party. They spoke to Mrs. Meeker first, and said, "How do you do," with a deep and pathetic emphasis. They then shook hands with us until our hearts burned. One of the men said, "Can you give us a description of your captivity?" and we sat down and had a talk. The Utes all laughed at us. We did not have but a few minutes of conversation for fear it would not be good for us. Mrs. Meeker was talking with Gen. Adams. He said she looked as if she was starved. He gave her a piece of cracker and some ————. The Indians had already opened the cans but knowing what they were looked on with surprise but they ate all the canned food and got away with some blankets.

In regard to my days of captivity I can only say the Indians were at times lively and joked with us, so that I was forced to laugh, a good many times at their strange humor when I did not feel like it. It seemed to please them very much. They would say "————— good woman." When Josephine came in they would say she was cross. She was very much grieved and when her blood was up she talked to them in a lively strain and made them treat Mrs. Meeker better. After Johnson and Mrs. Meeker had talked together about the Agent, Mrs. Meeker came to Johnson's to stay. He treated her with great care. Previously she was not welcomed. The meanest thing they did to the poor little woman was to frighten her with their knives and horrible grimaces and bad stories. They tried to scare her out of her wits.

I think Douglas is the worst of the Indians. Jack is pretty mean also — mean enough for any purpose, no matter how bad. Johnson is the best. Johnson's wife was very kind. She treated me just like a mother, though sometimes when tired she would order me to get water. She treated my little girl very kindly, made moccasins for her, and grieved over her and my boy as if they were her own. She said the Utes had killed the child's papa. "Utes no good." She was for peace. She was Chief Ouray's sister and Ouray was friendly to the whites and had sent messages to her that the whites were not to be abused, and should be returned soon.

The Indians laid all the blame on Mr. Meeker. They said he brought the soldiers in and would have Jack, Pauvits, Douglas and other chiefs, including Johnson, taken up for stealing and put in the calaboose. They said Meeker made great pictures of his being shot and had sent them to Washington. The Indians said they had found these pictures on Thornburgh's body, that they had been sent by Meeker to inflame the soldiers as the pictures represented the treatment the agency employees would receive from the Indians and the soldiers must come to prevent it.

After we were released we stopped all night at Johnson's camp and started early the next morning on ponies for the wagons, which had been left at the end of the road, about forty miles south of the Uncompahgre River. Gen. Adams had left us and gone to see the soldiers so Captain Cline was in charge of the party and our escort to the wagons on the way back. The Indians had accompanied us for a time, left us, and Captain Cline grew suspicious.

Captain Cline reached the wagons in a short time and as he suspected, found the Indians seated around the wagons in a body with most of the blankets, lying on the ground and divided among them. They had also gotten out the boxes of provisions and canned fruit which Gen. Adams had brought from Los Pinos for us. They had burst them open and were eating the contents. Captain Cline is personally acquainted with many of the Indians and he completely astonished them. Jumping off his horse he threw the reins on the ground and rushing forward in great anger he shouted: "Chief Ouray shall hear of this, and will settle with you."

He picked up an axe and began to split kindling wood to prepare for the captives. His object was to keep the axe in his hands and be master of the situation until the main party should arrive. He feared treachery and putting on a bold front he made it pretty lively for the Indians. They fell back, got all the blankets and gave up the canned fruit. Captain Cline threw the blankets on the wagons with what canned provisions were left. Shortly after this occurrence we arrived with Mr. Sherman. We then traveled on to Chief Ouray's home.

Captain Cline was met by Ouray at the gate. The good chief looked at him a moment and said:

"Captain, tell me how you found things when you reached the wagons."

The Captain was surprised, narrated the facts as I have stated. Chief Ouray listened a moment and grimly smiling, said:

"Yes, you reached the wagons at such a time and you found Utes around the wagons eating fruit. I know all about it. Ouray not a fool. I had good and true brothers in the mountains around the wagons. They look down and see bad Indians, and then when wagons start safely the good Indians run back to Ouray on fast horses and tell Ouray, and Ouray make up his mind about it. Bad Utes can't fool Ouray."

The chief said this in broken English to the Captain, but, when he spoke to Mr. Pollock he conversed in eloquent and pretentious Spanish, for he had been educated among the Spanish-Mexicans of Taos, down on the border, and his words are always delivered with great fluency.

We were all treated well at Ouray's home. It had Brussels carpet, window curtains, stoves, good beds, glass windows, rocking chairs, camp woods, mirrors and an elegantly carved bureau. We were received as old and long lost friends. Mrs. Ouray wept for our hardships, and her motherly face, dusky but beautiful with sweetness and compassion, was wet with tears. We left her crying. From this point we took the United States mail coaches, with fleet horses and expert drivers. The journey over the lofty mountains for three days and one night brought us out of the San Juan country to the swiftly flowing Rio Grande. The Indian Reservation was seventy miles behind us. Two ranges of mountains lay between us and that captivity of terror. We could not forget the noble Ouray and his true friends who lived there, yet it made our tired hearts beat rapturously when we saw the steam cars at Alamosa.

Flora R. Price

Denver, Colo.
October 31st, 1879.

Mrs. Meeker and her daughter Rozene. This picture, taken many years after Mrs. Meeker's ordeal while in captivity, shows a face lined with pain and suffering.

Courtesy Greeley Municipal Museum

Photo of the White River Museum located in Meeker, Colorado. Iva Kendall, Curator, is shown near doorway. The museum is housed in one of the original buildings which made up the U.S. Army post, built after the Meeker Massacre.

Photo by Author

Photo of plow used at the Agency, to plow the Indian pasture-lands. This was one of the reasons that the Utes rebelled against Meeker. Plow and other Meeker relics may be seen in the White River Museum.

Photo by Author

CHAPTER NINE

Aftermath

Interestingly enough, all three of the women captives failed to make any mention in their stories as to whether they had been sexually abused by their captors. General Adams had interviewed all three of the women and they had denied any such abuse by the Indian men. Later, when the women were at Chief Ouray's home, they were interviewed again — this time by Inspector William J. Pollock. After the interviews, he sent the following note to Commissioner Hayt:

October 29, 1879

Commissioner Hayt:

I have also a statement given to me personally and in confidence of a character too delicate to mention here as to the personal treatment they severally received from the Indians during captivity.

This has been one of the roughest trips I ever made and am suffering intensly with rheumatism. Expect to reach the Southern Ute Agency day after tomorrow.

Wm. J. Pollock.

Inspector

When General Adams received this information he made the trip to Greeley, accompanied by a secretary and again interviewed Arvilla and Josephine Meeker and Mrs. Price. They admitted that their first stories were untrue, but felt justified due to the publicity they would have received. After their ordeal, they had been both ashamed and afraid to tell the true story. Now they admitted that they had been outraged by the Indians.

General Adams and General Hatch then formed the Ute Commission which was to investigate — not only the massacre but also the Indian abuse of the captive women.

Let us digress for a moment and mention a few other incidents connected with the return of the erstwhile captives to Greeley. The tumultous welcome that awaited Arvilla, Josephine and Mrs. Price was probably one of the greatest moments experienced by the people of Greeley. In keeping with this outward manifestation by the people of Greeley, a testimonial letter was also sent to Mrs. Meeker, which read as follows:

Dear Mrs. Meeker:

The people of Greeley have mourned sincerely and deeply with you for the death of your honored husband. We have unanimously defended his good name, and will proclaim the spirit of benevolence and generosity towards the Indians with which he accepted the responsibilities and entered upon the work to which the government called him. We recognize the carefullness and discretion shown in choosing his employees, all of whom justified his selection by their competence, activity and fidelity to him and his plans. We cannot too highly commend his goodness of purpose, his strict obedience to the instructions of the government, his rigid faithfulness to it, to his convictions of duty and to his cherished determination to deal justly by and to improve his miserable and ungrateful wards.

We have been anxious and distressed for you and your companions in your trial, and in the perils and hardships of captivity. Some among us prayed daily for you, and gave thanks when we heard of your recovery from the savages.

We have admired with enthusiasm the brave, womanly and noble spirit of your heroic daughter as her conduct has been reported to us.

In reverant remembrance of your husband, the founder of our colony, whose name is associated with its history to its honor, the honest man, the faithful citizen and officer of the government, and with high esteem for yourself — we desire to assure you of our deep sympathy and of our hearty welcome back to your home and to us. While we have been perplexed by what means we might best express our sympathy and our welcome, we heartily pledge you whatever we can to comfort your sorrow and to help your future to be happy.

Joseph Moore and Wife
F.L. Childs and Wife
A.K. Packard and Wife
B.H. Yerkes and Wife

In response to this letter, the Meekers replied as follows:

To Messers, White, Moore, Childs, Packard, Yerkes, and Wives:

Dear Friends — No words can express our gratitude for the

Photo of items relating to the Meeker Massacre. Arvilla Meeker's sewing machine is shown in front center. The Indians apparently took it along with them but dropped it along the trail, as they retreated from the pursuing soldiers, after the massacre.

Photo by Author

Photo of items dealing with the Meeker Massacre and associated events. Rifle and pipe, shown in photo, belonged to Chief Colorow, who fought the soldiers at Milk Creek. Major Thornburgh's picture is shown in upper center. (White River Museum)

Photo by Author

deep, unspeakable heart-sympathy which you have shown us in so many ways. We rejoice to be with you again — to walk in these pleasant streets, and to greet you at your firesides. A few weeks ago this was a dream. We thought we should never see your faces again. But Heaven be praised, we are back in this dear town once more — here in Greeley where we hope to live and end our days with you. Dear friends, your dedicacy, your generosity, your honorable sorrow for those who can be with us here no more touch us too deeply for further utterance.

    With sincere thanksgiving we sign ourselves,

Arvilla D. Meeker

Josephine Meeker

Flora Ellen Price

    In addition, Ralph Meeker, the son of Nathan C. Meeker, sent the following communication to the people of Greeley:

Greeley, Colorado, Nov. 3, 1879

To the Press and People of Colorado:

My mother, Mrs. N.C. Meeker, her daughter Josephine, and Mrs. Price wish to express their profound gratitude to the people and press of this State for the sympathy and hospitality which have been so spontaneously and universally shown them since their escape from captivity. In Denver, Greeley, Colorado Springs, Pueblo, Alamosa, Lake City, Ouray, Los Pinos, and at all the stage stations along the route of return for 500 miles, the most tender and respectful attention was shown them.

    As a son of the murdered Agent and as a journalist, I denounce the ignorance and disgraceful incompetency of those newspapers which are accusing my father of cruelty to the Indians. Their assertions and their arguments are simply rubbish and unworthy of true journalism. N.C. Meeker was a graduate of Oberlin College, he was born and raised in the Western Reserve of Ohio; he was a confidential friend and personal admirer of Horace Greeley. He believed in justice to all men, white, red or black — Christian or infidel. But the Chicago Interior disgraces the Christianity it professes, trails its journalistic pretentions in the mud by echoing the malicious statement of Charles A. Davis that my father robbed the Indians of their pasture lands. These are the facts: The old agency had just been moved to a new and unoccupied place, selected by my father as an agent of the Government. It was he, not the Indians who moved there though he went by their assistance and consent. They helped move the agency and erect the buildings, and then when he was established, they pitched their tents at his door, and the woman Jane discovered that the plowing might interfere with the pasturage of her ponies. My father at once called a council of the Indians, accepted new conditions by which the absurd claim was relinquished. The Indians said they were satisfied and there was no more complaint until the one man Johnson came in from the woods and began to find fault. But for arguments sake I will admit for ten minutes that I am a liar, that my father was an oppressor, that Douglas, Johnson, Jane and co., were as immaculate as the editor of the Chicago Interior — while I ask this question: Why did Chief Ouray denounce the massacre; why did his wife rise up in the night and denounce the murders as her husband told me she did. By the words of the noblest of all the Utes, by the words of his wife Chepeta, who cried like a child over the agency butchery, by the words of Henry Jim and all honest Utes the editor of the Christian Interior newspaper of Chicago and Charles Davis to go west and start a little agency of their own.

Ralph Meeker.

To further show the respect and esteem in which Nathan C. Meeker was held in Greeley, the Board of Town Trustees, passed the following resolutions.

Greeley, Colo., Nov. 4, 1879
At a regular meeting of the Board of Town Trustees, held at Town Hall, Nov. 3, 1879, the following preamble and resolution having been introduced by Trustee A.Z. Salomon, were on motion unanimously passed and adopted by the Board, to wit:

That in order to communicate the meritorious services of Hon. N.C. Meeker, the father of the Union Colony of Colorado, and the founder of our Town, and who as the agent of the White River Agency was massacred by the Ute India is on or about the 29th day of September, A.D., 1879.

Therefore be it

Resolved, That the name of Main St., in the Town of Greeley, be and is hereby changed and that the name be called for the future Meeker Avenue, and it is further

Resolved, That the Recorder be instructed to procure a first-class portrait, in oil painting, of Father Meeker, to be placed in the Town Hall of our town.

On motion of Trustee L.B. Willard, the foregoing preamble,

and resolutions were ordered to be published in the town papers.

W.C. Sanders, Mayor.

Attest, L.Von Gohren, Recorder.

It seems that no portrait of Mr. Meeker was ever procured by the Town administrator, however. Main street was never changed to Meeker Avenue. It was changed to "Eighth Street," and today, it is known as Eighth Avenue.

About a year after the massacre, Meeker's body was brought to Greeley and buried in Linn Grove Cemetery. Despite efforts to raise the sum of $1,000 for a monument at his grave, the donations never reached this figure and consequently no monument was provided by the citizens of Greeley. Mrs. Meeker finally contracted to have a Scotch granite monument erected at her husband's grave.

Author's Note: The inscription on the monument shows that besides Mr. and Mrs. Meeker being buried there, the following names of their children, who are also buried there, are inscribed on the monument at Linn Grove Cemetery, in Greeley:

Nathan Cook Meeker

Arvilla Meeker

George Meeker

Josephine Meeker

Mary A. Meeker Fullerton

Ralph Meeker

Rozene Meeker

What about punishment for those Utes who had committed the massacre? In order to investigate the massacre, the Interior Department appointed a commission consisting of Generals Hatch and Adams, along with Chief Ouray. Negotiations were to open at the Los Pinos Agency. The idea was to get the Utes to turn in those who had participated in the massacre. The Commission members were agreed that the Thornburgh fight was a regular battle and none of the Utes who participated in it were to be punished. However, those who had taken part in killing innocent, unarmed men at the Agency, should be placed on trial and punished, if proven guilty.

There was one hitch — none of the Indians would testify that they knew anything about the massacre, or identify those who participated. The captive women, (Arvilla, Josephine, and Mrs. Price) had named twelve Indians who had participated in the massacre.

Meeker gravesite in Linn Grove Cemetery in Greeley, Colorado. The large granite marker is flanked by a flagpole which was placed there honoring Nathan C. Meeker. Mr. and Mrs. Meeker and their five children are all buried here.

Photo by Author

Generals Hatch and Adams, tired of the Indians' stalling tactics, now ordered Chief Ouray to have these twelve men brought in for trial.

Chief Ouray informed Adams and Hatch that the twelve Indians would be delivered only if they were to be tried in Washington. He felt they would not be given a fair trial in Colorado. Hatch replied that they would accept the offer to bring in the twelve men and he would contact Secretary Schurz about having the trial in Washington.

Chiefs Jack and Colorow were then sent off by Ouray to find the camp of the hostiles and bring them in. These two chiefs were exonerated for their part in the Thornburgh fight. They were unable to bring in the twelve Utes, with the exception of Douglas.

Eventually, some of the murderers were sent to Washington but nothing was done to them. Douglas was sent to Fort Leavenworth. He was later set free and died of insanity, not long after.

Feelings were still running high among the people of Colorado. They wanted the Utes punished for the Meeker Massacre. Furthermore, their cry of "The Utes Must Go," became increasingly louder and more insistent.

Chief Ouray and Secretary Carl Schurz worked incessantly to hammer out a treaty that would be acceptable to both Whites and Indians. Chief Ouray knew that his own days were numbered, due to poor health. He was anxious to conclude the treaty agreement before he passed on. While he was a staunch friend of the whites, he never forgot his obligations to his own people — obligations assumed when he became the chief of all the Utes.

The agreement was finally ready for Senate and tribal ratification. It provided for the following:

1. The White River Utes would be moved to the southern part of the Uintah Reservation in Utah.

2. Moving the Southern Utes thirty miles west from their lands below Pagosa Springs, and reducing their acreage by a third.

3. Placing the Uncompahgre Utes on lands around the Grand River, Gunnison River junction.

The Utes ratified the agreement before the year 1880 came to a close. Chief Ouray designated Chief Sapovanero as his successor and the treaty terms proceeded smoothly. It was discovered however, that the Gunnison-Grand region did not have enough agricultural lands so the new Uncompahgre Reservation was placed on a Utah tract, running along the Green River for twenty-five miles beyond its junction with the White River.

On September 1, 1881, General Mackenzie began moving the White River Utes on their 350 mile trip to their Utah Reservation. There were 1,458 Ute men, women and children; 8,000 ponies; 10,000 sheep and goats, plus all of their belongings which were carried on pack trains. Some of the Utes went reluctantly, but Mackenzie threatened to seize their guns and belongings, so this problem was finally settled.

Chief Ouray lived to see his Utes given a chance to live in harmony among the Whites. His death came on August 24, 1880. Chief Jack, who had refused to go to the Uintah Reservation, worked as a teamster on the Rawlins-Fort Washakie road. He was

Chief Ouray was a good friend of the whites but at the same time never forgot his obligations to his own people — the Ute Indians.

Sketch by Jack Henderson

killed while resisting arrest on April 29, 1882. He was to have been arrested and questioned about stealing a horse. Chief Colorow died in his camp on White River on December 11, 1888.

In retrospect, what really caused the White River Utes to rise up against Meeker, knowing that he represented the government of the United States? Many reasons have been given but it was probably a combination of things and happenings that kept building up until a breaking point was reached.

Let us now consider some of the grievances enumerated by the White River Utes — some of which dealt with Meeker while others were against the government:

1. Refusal to sell the Utes guns and ammunition at the agency. The Agent and the government felt that the Indians should learn to farm and give up hunting. The Indians needed guns to hunt, and had to buy guns and ammunition from off-agency traders at inflated prices.

2. Failure to pay the Indians money that was owed them for the cession of their lands.

3. Failure of the government to live up to treaty stipulations.

4. Failure to make up arrears in annuity payments.

5. Rumor that the government was proposing to move the Utes to a reservation in the hated Indian Territory.

6. The Utes did not want to be forced to send their children to school. They were afraid also that by educating their young people, the old lifestyle of the Indians would disappear.

7. The Utes did not want to work. The warriors felt work was for squaws. Agent Meeker kept harping to them about work.

8. The White River Utes never seemed to like Agent Meeker. He was a man who lived by rules and regulations and expected his Indian charges to do likewise.

When the Utes resisted his efforts to force them to give up their way of life and become farmers, he threatened to bring in the soldiers, arrest them and possibly put them in jail.

The final blow came when Meeker sent for the troops. When the troops crossed the reservation boundary, the Indians took this as a declaration of war and promptly attacked Thornburgh's troops. At the same time, they killed Meeker and his employees, as an act of revenge for all the injustices they felt had been perpetrated against them. The attack on the Agency was also in retaliation for the attack on the Indians at Milk Creek.

One can only speculate that if the bloodshed could have been avoided, and Utes allowed to retain at least a portion of their beloved homelands in Colorado — would not the Utes, over a period of time, adapted themselves to living in harmony with a changing civilization? Prior to the time of the Meeker Massacre, many of the Utes were already adapting well to the new life and as a general rule, getting along well with their white neighbors.

Let us continue our speculation. Perhaps the massacre would never have taken place if the following conditions had been met:

1. Meeker should not have been such a strict and unbending disciplinarian with the Indians. Rev. Danforth, who had been the previous Agent at White River, had accomplished a great deal during his four-year term there. He had been more understanding of the Utes and had tried to help them in a friendly and cooperative way.

2. The Agent should not have threatened the Indians in the manner that he did. Perhaps the government should have heeded the warning signs and replaced him before the situation got out of hand.

3. By calling in the troops, Meeker sealed his own doom. Had the government sent a negotiation team to the Agency, perhaps a workable solution could have been worked out.

Nathan C. Meeker will never be forgotten. The town of Meeker, Colorado, located four miles east of the former White River Agency, was named in his honor by the townspeople. The City of Greeley, likewise stands as an enduring monument to his dedicated efforts in leading the early colonists through trying times, in order to establish the rich farming area that he envisioned. This area now exceeds even Meeker's fondest expectations — businesses, homes, farms, resort areas, and much more. It seems fitting and appropriate to quote the following prophetic passage from one of Mr. Meeker's articles — an article that appeared in the first issue of the Greeley Tribune, dated November 16, 1870:

"Individuals may rise and fall — may live or die — property may be lost or gained; but the colony as a whole will prosper and the spot on which we labor shall, so long as the world stands, be the center of intelligence and activity. Great social reforms leading to the elevation of mankind move as if directed by destiny. It is the vast future more than the brief present, that is to be benefited; hence sympathies and feelings are of little moment, and the cause moves on as if animated by a cold life of its own."

Chief Colorow and his Utes were moved to Utah in September, 1881. He died on December 11, 1888, at his camp on the White River.

Sketch by Jack Henderson

APPENDIX A

Copy of a letter written by Fred Shepard to his father, George L. Shepard, in Greeley, Colorado. Fred Shepard, a youth of twenty years, was hired as a carpenter by Nathan C. Meeker to work at the White River Agency in the spring of 1879. The letter was written on June 2, 1879, and tells of his work on the agency buildings — moving them from a former location to a location in the meadow close to what is now the town of Meeker.

Fred Shepard was killed at the agency on September 29, 1879, along with Meeker and the other agency employees, by the White River Ute Indians.

White River, Colo June 3/79

Dear Father

I recd. yours of May 23 in due time and was glad to hear from you as you may know. I wrote a letter to Ruby last Sunday, and was pitching quoits the rest of the day and didn't "get to write". I have been laying floor today and putting in windows and door casings. Have been at work for over a week tearing down and moving a big log house, about thirty-five feet by sixteen and a 16 by 16 foot ell. Have got all the logs up now and part of the roof on the rest is at the old agency yet and one team up there now for a load. I was up there two or three days last week tearing down the building. I was surprised to see what a lot of buildings there is up there. A good steam sawmill, shingle mill etc. We have not got started on the logs that were cut last winter but we are liable to have to start them down before long, but hardly believe I will have to help drive them. He seems to have lots of carpenter work for me to do. Perhaps you will think it is no big job to tear down a log house of that dimension and haul it 12 miles and put it up again just as it was. It is a nice building at least it was once the logs are all hewn, to about 8" inches thick and morticed in to upright posts in several places as you see the logs were not long enough to reach. They are all cottonwood. I wish you could get me about two good towells and send them in by mail in here now so it don't matter when you write, we will soon have the P.O. down here too but now we have to go to the old Agency after our mail.

We are a little south of west of Greeley, don't know the altitude but it is some higher than Greeley. We had a little snow squall last week had two days of cold rainy weather. Will help the crops wonderfully.

June 5 noon. Part of the boys have gone up to the old place for lumber and part are out butchering. Price and I are the only ones here to dinner. N.C.'s family have got moved down here now. I am at work on the house right along. Will go above Monday and commence tearing down another building. I hear ————— Fullerton, Geo Eaton and another man are on the way in here. Don't know how true it is. The boys used to plague Joe, they called him the "fondling" is the reason he didn't like to stay here but it is good enough for me, and if things go along as they are now I shall probably stay some time but I am afraid if he gets all of the Greeleyites out here the Department won't like it and discharge about half of us. I was in hopes that I could wait for my box until I got some money but I guess you may send it as soon as possible. There will be some teams leave Rawlins in a short time for here and they can bring it if you will direct it (in care of James France) Rawlins, Wy T.) Yes I will want a couple of pairs of taps and some pegs and an assortment of awls, crooked sewing and pegging. Bert has got a handle so you needn't send one. About a half a dozen good big towels. You may send one by mail as I am in need of one. Send my razor outfit, toothbrush, and a little bunch of toothpicks in my valise. I would like it if I had some flannel shirts too. Besides overalls stockings, shirts and overalls is the main thing here. Can't get buckskin breeches here any better than in Greeley unless we make them and it is a big job. Bert's folks will want to send some things ————— until into July some time but you shall have all I have left after my board bill is paid here and I get a pair of moccasins apiece for Ruby and I. I have ordered a pair made for Ruby with beads all over them, of Jane . Will send them to her by mail as soon as they are done. I wrote a long letter to her last week and I guess this will wear you out so I will close, From your affectionate son, Fred.

———————————————————

This letter was saved by Fred's father and later given to his sister, Ruby Shepard. The letter later ended up with Ruby's daughter, Florence McClave Barton of Williamsport, Pennsylvania. The letter is now in the White River Museum, located in Meeker, Colorado.

APPENDIX B

Appendix B contains copies of several letters, dealing with the Thornburgh Battle on Milk Creek. The first letter was addressed to Lieutenant Samuel A. Cherry by some of the men who served under him at the battle on Milk Creek, on September 29, 1879, and goes as follows:

November 21, 1879

2nd Lieut. Samuel A. Cherry,
     5th Cavalry

Sir:

We, the undersigned Non-commissioned officers of Company E 3rd Cavalry and Companies "D" and "F", 5th Cavalry, desire to express to you our admiration of the gallant and praiseworthy conduct displayed by you in the recent engagement with the Ute Indians at Milk River on September 29th, 1879.

To a brave man, bravery needs no better or higher reward than the consciousness of duty well performed, but in order that you should fully understand the feeling of approbation that exists among the men who fought with you, we take this method of tendering to you our hearty approval.

You do not need this — you have already made yourself a page in the history of our country and endeared yourself to the men who witnessed your noble conduct, and who feel that to a great extent it is to your coolness and sagacity, they owe their lives. The party that accompanied you on your dangerous mission to check the enemy and cover the retreat, knew full well that the chances of life and death were unequally paired, and that one false move would turn the scale far down on the side of death. But, you did not make that move. With unflinching courage you held the Indians in check though their bullets were striking your men from every side, and by your bearing, nerved even the wounded to fight to the last — and when the retreat was safely made, and your services at that point no longer necessary — with seventeen of the twenty men composing your party, wounded, you accomplished your own retreat, fighting your way inch by inch, without leaving one of your wounded on the field.

Such conduct is beyond all praise. — No words of ours can express to you the respect we feel for the man who displayed such courage, — but if in the future it should be your lot to lead men on to some great feat of daring, as long as there remains a man who fought with you at Milk River you will find ready and willing hands to share your glory or your death.

But this is not all: — When the brunt of the fight was over — when each man looked about him, and saw the fearful destruction wrought — when each heart for the moment quailed at the thought of what the morrow might bring — when the excitement of the battle had passed and the reaction had brought dispair in its stead, you infused a new spirit in the hearts of the despairing men, and by the force of your example led them to make still greater efforts leading toward their own preservation and defence.

In conclusion we have only to add that we express the sentiments of the companies we represent and are proud to be permitted to do honor to one whom honor is richly due, — to a soldier among soldiers, a man among men.

Very Respectfully
Your Obdt. Servants
First Sergeant E.P. Grimes, Co. F 5 Cavy.

(Thirteen other non-commissioned officers signed, under the signature of Sergeant Grimes)

The second letter listed here, was a letter sent by Robert B. Grimes, Assistant Surgeon with the Milk Creek expedition, to the U.S. Surgeon General, Jos. K. Raines.

It is interesting to note that while most historical accounts of Major Thornburgh's death, state that he was killed by a bullet through his head, the following letter, filed in the U.S. Archives, states otherwise. The letter follows:

Camp of Ute Expedition
Milk River, Colorado
Sept. 30th. 1879

Surgeon General Jos. K. Raines, U.S.A.
Washington, D.C.
General:

I have the honor to inform you of the death of Major T.T. Thornburgh, 4th U.S. Infantry in the action of the 29th inst. fought between three companies of cavalry and the hostile Ute Indians, on Milk Creek, Colorado. The immediate cause of death, was a gunshot wound of chest, the ball passing from left to right, through both lungs.

I have the honor to be, General,

Very respectfully,
Your ob't Serv't
Robert B. Grimes
Act. Asst. Surgeon,
with Ute Expedition.

BIBLIOGRAPHY
(Books)

Boyd, David. A History: Greeley And The Union Colony Of Colorado. The Greeley Tribune Press. Greeley, Colo., 1890.

Bourke, John G. On The Border With Crook. Glorieta, New Mexico. The Rio Grande Press, Inc., 1969.

Brininstool, E.A. Fighting Indian Warriors. Harrisburg, Penn., The Stackpole Company. 1953.

Brown, Dee. Bury My Heart At Wounded Knee. New York, Holt, Rinehart and Worster. 1971.

Clark, J. Max. Colonial Days. The Smith-Brooks Company, Denver, Colo. 1902.

Dawson, Thomas F., and Skiff, F.J.V. The Ute War. Johnson Publishing Company. 1980.

Dunn, J.P. Jr., Massacres Of The Mountains. Archer House, Inc., New York. 1979.

Emmitt, Robert. The Last War Trail. University Of Oklahoma Press. Norman. 1954.

Geffs, Mary L. Under Ten Flags. Self-Published. Greeley, Colo. 1938.

Hyde, George F. Indians Of The High Plains. University Of Oklahoma Press. Norman. 1959.

King, Charles. Campaigning With Crook. Harper and Brothers. New York. 1890.

Look, Al. Utes Last Stand. Golden Bell Press. Denver, Colo. 1972.

Longstreet, Stephen. War Cries On Horseback. Garden City, New York. Doubleday and Co., Inc. 1970.

McClellan, Val J. This Is Our Land, Volume 1. Vantage Press, Inc. New York, N.Y. 1977.

McClellan, Val J. This Is Our Land, Volume 2. Western Publishers. Jamestown, Ohio. 1979.

Mumey, Nolie. The Ute War. Johnson Publishing Company. Boulder, Colo. 1964.

Marshall, S.L.A., Crimsoned Prairie. Charles Scribner's Sons. New York. 1972.

Mills, Anson. My Story. Self-Published. Washington, D.C. 1918.

Rankin, M. Wilson. Reminiscences Of Frontier Days. Self-Published. Boulder, Colo. 1935.

Sprague, Marshall. Massacre — The Tragedy At White River. University of Nebraska Press. Lincoln. 1957.

Urquhart, Lena M. Colorow: The Angry Chieftain. Golden Bell Press. Denver, Colo. 1968.

Utley, Robert M. and Wilcomb E. Washburn. The Indian Wars. American Heritage Publishing Company. New York. 1977.

Vaughn, J.W. Indian Fights: New Facts On Seven Encounters. University of Oklahoma Press. Norman. 1966.

— ARTICLES —

Certificate Of Capt. J. Scott Payne, 5th U.S. Cavalry, Concerning Loss And Destruction Of Train And Supplies At Battle On Milk River, Colorado, September 29th, 1879. Annals Of Wyoming, Volume 3, No. 1, pp. 137-144.

"Major Thompson, Chief Ouray and the Utes," by Thomas F. Dawson. The Colorado Magazine, Volume 7, No. 3, May 1930, pp. 113-122.

"The Meeker Massacre," by M. Wilson Rankin. Annals of Wyoming, Volume 16, No. 2, pp. 87-145, July 1944.

"The Meeker Massacre," by Marshall D. Moody. Colorado Magazine, Volume 30, No. 2, pp. 91-104, April 1953.

"Terror At White River," Colorful Colorado, Volume 3, No. 1, Summer, 1967.

"Fort Fred Steele: Desert Outpost On The Union Pacific," by Robert A. Murray. Annals of Wyoming, pp. 140-206, Fall 1972.

"The Thornburgh Battle With The Utes on Milk Creek," by Elmer R. Burkey. Colorado Magazine, Volume 13, No. 3, pp. 90-111, May 1936.

— NEWSPAPERS —

The Greeley Tribune, Greeley, Colorado — October & November 1879

The Rocky Mountain News — October 7, 1879

The Denver Post — Denver, Colorado. October 1935

The New York Tribune — New York. 1879

The New York Herald — New York. 1879

— GOVERNMENT PUBLICATIONS —

United Service — Military And Naval Affairs — "Incidents Of The Recent Campaign Against The Utes." Volume II, Jan.-June, 1880, pp. 114-129.

Journal Of The United States Cavalry Association. "The Outbreak Of September, 1879, by H.W. Spooner. pp. 1125-1128, May 1910.

Annual Report Of The Commissioner Of Indian Affairs To The Secretary Of The Interior For The Year 1879. Washington, D.C., Government Printing Office, 1879.

Official Records and Reports, The National Archives, Washington, D.C.

PART TWO

RECENT RESEARCH AT THE THORNBURGH BATTLE SITE AND MEEKER MASSACRE SITE

INTRODUCTION

The author's research at the sites mentioned above, was conducted during 1983 and 1984. In all, a total of ten trips were made during this period — trips from Greeley, Colorado to Meeker, Colorado, generally of several days duration.

The author used a metal detector in looking for battlefield relics and to establish where the ebb and flo of action took place. Cameras were used to take the black and white, color, and color slides of the historical points, which photos will appear in this book. A cassette recorder was also used in interviewing persons who had a knowledge of the historical sites as well as for background information.

Part One of this book is the story of the Meeker Massacre and Thornburgh Battle, according to the best historical accounts available. Part Two consists of "on the site research," which the author hopes will give the reader a feeling of "I was there." In a sense, the reader is there, as he follows the author into the field and experiences the same thrill as the author did, when he unearthed the battlefield relics.

History can be a living thing — enriching our lives as we experience the happenings of long ago. We can share the same sorrow, despair, and anxiety — as well as the same hopes and dreams that the participants of these events experienced. Then history will have truly fulfilled its mission.

CHAPTER TEN

Meeker Massacre Research — 1983-1985

Trip No. 1

July 12, 1983 — I had been wanting to go to the Meeker Massacre historical site for some time. In discussing it with two friends — John Wheeler and Dr. John Fulbright, it was decided to make the trip together. I had visited with them on a number of occasions and told them about my research at various historical sites. They wanted to participate since Wheeler had two metal detectors and wanted to try them out at an historical battle site.

We left Greeley on Tuesday, July 12, at 6:00 A.M. It was a clear, warm day. We drove to Ft. Collins and then up the Poudre River Canyon and then over Cameron Pass. We arrived at Walden at 9:00 A.M. and had our breakfast there.

Continuing on our trip we drove to Steamboat Springs, Craig, and finally arrived at Meeker, Colorado at 1:00 P.M. It had warmed up considerably since we had left Greeley. After having lunch and reserving motel rooms, we headed for the Thornburgh Battle site, which was located about nineteen miles from town. About fifteen miles of this was over a dirt road and this part of the drive was very dusty and hot.

I had given my two companions copies of a small map which detailed the main landmarks of the Thornburgh Battlefield. When we arrived at the site, we took pictures of the historical markers that had been placed near the road. We then looked at our maps and identified some of the places where the action took place. I decided to climb a steep hill to the south of Milk Creek while my two companions headed for several hills to the north of the creek. The battle account stated that the Utes had held these hills and fired on the soldiers who had barricaded themselves within their circled wagon train.

I sweated profusely under the hot July sun as I climbed the hill. On reaching the top, I found that it was covered by a heavy growth of sagebrush, chokecherry bushes, and other vegetation. Hardly an ideal place to work with a metal detector. Near the highest point of this hill, I found a lone cartridge case from a Henry rifle — one of the rifle types used by the Indians. We had only a few hours to work since we got a very larte start, having agreed beforehand that we would meet at the car by 5:30 P.M.

When I met my two companions, they eagerly asked me if I had found anything. They were quite excited when I showed them my find. They had not found anything but some pieces of iron, wire, and other junk. That is the way things go however, in researching for battle relics — it is persistence that counts.

We drove back to Meeker and decided to drive several miles west of town, where there are several roadside markers telling about the Meeker Massacre. There is one marker that points southward towards a monument in a hayfield, close to the White River. This is where the White River Indian Agency buildings stood and also where Mr. Meeker and his employees were killed by the Utes on September 29, 1879.

We took more pictures and then drove to our motel. After a refreshing shower, we went out for dinner. We all went to bed early that night because the long, hot day had exhausted us.

July 13, 1983 — We had decided to get an early start today, work until about noon and then start back on our return trip to Greeley. After breakfast, we again headed back for the Thornburgh Battle site.

A few explanatory comments may be in order at this time, concerning the Thornburgh Battle. Nathan C. Meeker, the Indian Agent at the White River Agency, had asked the government to send troops because he felt things were getting out of hand at the Agency. The Utes were becoming increasingly more belligerent. As a result, Major Thornburgh with about 150 men set out from Ft. Steele to go to the Agency and try to straighten things out between the Agent and the Indians.

As the troops neared Milk Creek, the Indians became increasingly alarmed and warned that they would fight if the soldiers crossed Milk Creek, which was the boundary line of the Ute Reservation. In fact, the Indians prepared an ambush in the Milk Creek area. Here the creek runs through a small valley, bounded on both sides by a series of high hills. This is where the Utes positioned themselves, and, as the battle developed, they fired at the soldiers who had sought refuge in their circled wagon train.

Now back to our research — we arrived at the site at 8:30 A.M. I forgot to mention that we had stopped at the William Squire ranch and obtained permission to use our metal detectors at the battle site.

I decided to work a long hill on the north side of Milk Creek and John Wheeler decided to accompany me. Dr. Fulbright decided to work another hill, to our left. I climbed the western end of the hill and skipped the lower part, heading for the higher part of the hill. I found my first cartridge case — another Henry rifle case. Continuing along the crest of the hill I found three more Henry cases, one 45-70 case and one 54-70 case.

John Wheeler was a short distance below me and I could hear him yelling. He excitedly informed me that he had found some relics. When I checked with him later, he had found two Henry cases and two 45-70 slugs — no doubt fired at the Indians on the hill, by the soldiers below. I decided to go back over the same area that I had covered but a bit lower but found nothing else. Coming back down from the hill, I walked over a plowed field to my right and climbed still another hill. I didn't find anyting there but John Wheeler, who had followed along behind me, found a 45-70 cartridge case.

We stopped working at 12:15 P.M. and returned to the car. It was another very hot day and since we were all very tired, decided to quit for the day. We drove to Craig where we had our lunch. Then drove to Steamboat Springs, Walden, and Ft. Collins, where we had supper. We then drove on to Greeley arriving there at 9:00 P.M.

The distance between Greeley and Meeker is about 275 miles and is a very picturesque drive. Rabbit Ears pass is especially beautiful, and the view one gets from the mountains coming into Steamboat Springs is certainly awe-inspiring.

I found a total of seven cartridge cases while John Wheeler found two slugs and three cases. Dr. Fulbright was unable to find any relics. We all took numerous pictures and certainly enjoyed the trip. I plan on making many more trips to the Meeker and Thornburgh sites in order to gather more material for my book which I hope to write about the Meeker Massacre and the Thornburgh Battle.

Trip No. 2

August 11, 1983 — My second trip began when I left Greeley at 6:15 A.M. Weather signs pointed to another hot day. I arrived in Walden which is 127 miles from Greeley, at 9:00 A.M. Had breakfast and gassed up the car.

It was very hot as I arrived in Craig where I had lunch. I then continued my trip until I arrived at the turn-off which leads to the Thornburgh Battlefield area. This is about two miles from Meeker. I arrived at the site at 1:40 P.M. I had previously called William Squire, the ranch owner on whose ranch the site is located, and received permission to continue my research there.

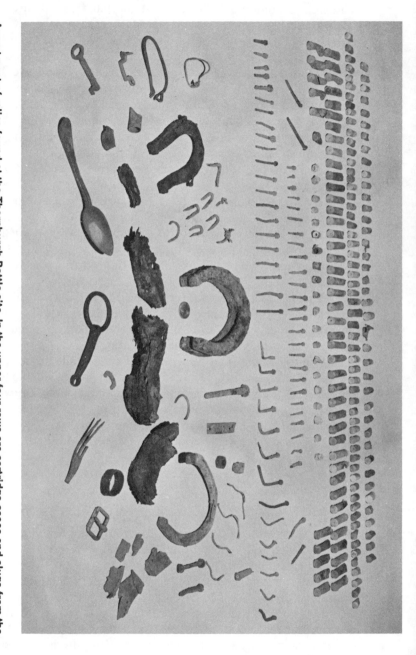

Assortment of relics found at the Thornburgh Battle site. In the upper four rows are cartridge cases and slugs from the rifles of the Indians and soldiers. Several rows of square-head nails follow. Bottom section of photo shows an army spoon, parts of a cavalryman's boot, horseshoes and parts of saddles, etc. The small coin shown between horseshoes in center of photo is an 1876 dime.

Photo by Bob Heiser

I started out by taking some slide picture of the historical markers and of the Milk Creek valley. Then I started up my metal detector and worked on the same hill where I had found cartridge cases on my previous trip. I found three pieces — two Henry rifle cases and one cartridge case, possibly a case fired from a Sharps rifle. These all came from the Indian rifles as they fired on the soldiers in the valley below them.

Reaching the end of the hill (east), I crossed over to an adjacent hill. This hill was slanted a bit in relation to the hill I had just covered. Although I worked the entire length of the hill's crest and part of the slope, I found nothing. Perhaps it was a bit too far away from the place where the soldiers were entrenched. The Indians apparently chose the closest points in order to produce a more effective rifle fire.

I continued metal-detecting on a hill adjacent to the high hill I had worked the last trip but found nothing there. It was now up in the 90 degree area and had clouded up, producing some thunder and lightning. With the weather threatening and since it was nearing 5:00 p.m., I decided to quit for the day and returned to Meeker. Checked in at the Gentry Motor Lodge. After I had cleaned up I noticed that it was raining quite hard outside. I drove to the Meeker historical marker west of town and then came back for supper.

During the evening I worked on my notes and also watched the TV news. I have no clearcut plan for tomorrow but need to take more pictures and slides in addition to looking for more relics.

August 12, 1983 — I could hear it raining outside all through the night. It was still quite cloudy in the morning but the rain had stopped. After breakfast, I visited the Meeker Library as well as the Museum. I checked out several books dealing with the Meeker Massacre.

Drove out to the Thornburgh Battle site and spent some time in taking slides. I had done some studying about the battle and remembered reading about a low hill which the soldiers held, early in the battle and before their retreat to the wagon train. A hill such as the one described lies north of the road and is about a half-mile from where the soldiers finally became entrenched. At first I didn't find anything on this hill. After I had metal-detected for about fifty yards, I got a good signal on my detector. It proved to be a 45-70 cartridge case, from a Springfield rifle (such as the soldiers used). I found a total of seventeen cartridge cases on this ridge, between 11:00 and 12:30 P.M.

After lunch I decided to try another low ridge on the south side of the road. I found only one 45-70 slug. I then drove to the spot where we found the cartridge cases on the first trip. This is about 150 yards north of Milk Creek. I decided to try the hill that was left of the plowed field, where we had previously found only one cartridge case.

On the highest point of the hill I found four Henry cartridge cases and one Sharps case. Returned to the car and rested a bit. Took a few more pictures and since it was getting late, I drove back to Meeker.

While I was having supper, I met a man who gave me the name of the ranch owner on which the White River Agency had been located and where Meeker and his employees were killed. Will contact him and try to get permission to go into the area for picture-taking and metal detecting. I also called William Squire and he offered to meet me at the Thornburgh site and show me around.

August 13, 1983 — I stopped by at the Squire Ranch, which is but a short distance from the Thornburgh site and had a nice visit with the Squire family. Mr. Squire had to take some diesel fuel to his haying rig so he told me to drive to the bridge at Milk Creek and he would meet me there as soon as he could.

After a short wait he met me there and pointed out the spot where Thornburgh and his men had placed their wagons in a circle and then fought off the Utes for five days, before help finally arrived. This area is now a barley field. Squire said that after the barley had been cut in September I could get in with my metal detector and work the area. He also informed me that various relics had been found in the field, in the past. This included army uniform buttons, shells, slugs, a spur, horseshoes, etc. The story goes that Thornburgh's silver mounted pistol is still somewhere in this field. He was killed while leading a charge to rescue some of his men who had been cut off by the Indians.

Squire then left me to go back to work. It was now 10:45 A.M. I had noticed another low hill, south of the road and about 300 to 400 yards above the ridge where I had found the 45-70's previously. This hill would have been about right for the Indians to shoot down at the soldiers, who were on the ridge below.

I climbed the hill and began working the lower end, closest to the road. I must have covered at least seventy-five yards before I got a signal on my metal detector. For the next hour-and-a-half, I was kept busy digging up Henry cartridge cases, and came up with a total of thirty-one. As I reached the southwestern part of the hill, there were no more cartridge cases to be found. This part of the hill sloped off in a different direction and was not near enough to the soldiers' position.

My plans had called leaving the area for home in the afternoon. Since it was already 1:00 P.M. I ate my lunch and then drove to Meeker for a gas refill. It was a cloudy but very warm day. I arrived at Ft. Collins at 7:00 P.M. and had supper there. Drove on to Greeley and arrived there at 8:30 P.M.

This second trip to the Meeker area gave me a much better insight into the battle and locations of the action. There are still a number of hills to check plus the barley field area. I tried contacting Aaron Woodward, on whose ranch the Agency was formerly located but was unable to reach him at home. Hope to see him on my next trip and get his permission to work the area where the Agency had originally stood and where the massacre occurred.

As I mentioned previously, there is a large granite stone and bronze marker about four miles west of Meeker. The inscription on the marker reads as follows:

"This native granite stone erected by the citizens of Rio Blanco County, Colorado — 1927

And dedicated to the memory of Nathan C. Meeker, United States Indian Agent, who with his government employees was massacred by the Ute Indians at the White River Ute Indian Agency, one and one-half miles west of this spot.

September 29, 1879.

Employees

W. H. Post	Frank Dresser
Henry Dresser	E.W. Eskridge
Mr. Price	
	Fred Shepard
George Eaton	Arthur L. Thompson
Carl Goldstein	Unknown Teamster

It is a sad commentary that Nathan C. Meeker had to die here, at the hands of the very people he was trying to help. All is quiet now on the hayfield that adjoins the White River — but on that fateful day of September 29, 1879, violence suddenly erupted and when it was over, Meeker and ten of his employees lay dead.

Trip No. 3

September 8, 1983 — It was a cool, clear morning when I left Greeley at 6:10 A.M. bound for Meeker again. I decided to drive awhile and have breakfast along the way. Arrived at Walden at

9:00 A.M. and had breakfast there. I continued my trip and drove straight through to Meeker, arriving there at 12:25 P.M. After checking in at the motel I had lunch and then headed for the Thornburgh Battle site.

It was fairly warm although clouds were still chasing across the sky. The sun shone intermittently. I arrived at the site at 2:00 P.M. and decided to work the Soldier Ridge first. This is the ridge that the soldiers held before retreating back to their wagons. I went rather quickly to the far end of the ridge which I hadn't really worked before. Between 2:00 and 5:30 P.M., I found the following items there:

> 11 — 45-70 cartridge cases
> 1 — 45-70 slug
> 1 — large chain
> 1 — small mule shoe

Drove back to Meeker and cleaned up before I went out for supper. After I returned to my motel, I called the owner of the ranch on which the Agency had stood but again could not reach him. He was out of town but his wife said she would have him call me when he got home. I was very tired and after finishing my notes I decided to call it a day and went to bed.

September 9, 1983 — I slept in this morning, probably due to the heavy day I had yesterday. After breakfast, I drove out to the battle site. It was partly cloudy but otherwise a nice day.

Arriving at the Thornburgh Battle site, I decided to work the hill south of the road, where I had found many Henry cartridge cases on my last trip. I started in at 9:30 A.M. and worked southward along the crest of the hill. At about 10:00 A.M. I found my first cartridge case for the day — a Henry case. From then on until noon, I was kept busy digging up cartridge cases.

I found the following items:

> 33 — Henry cartridge cases
> 2 — 45-70 cartridge cases
> 1 — unidentified case, about an inch long

Returned to the car for lunch. It had gotten quite windy and heavy clouds were setting in with a possibility of rain. I rested for a bit after lunch and then climbed a hill south of the road and across from the Thornburgh Battle site. This hill fronts toward the Milk Creek valley where the soldiers were holed up, but I could find nothing there.

There is another long hill, west of where I had been working. It is about three-quarters of a mile west of where the soldiers were entrenched. Jeff Squire, a son of ranch owner William Squire, told me that some of the old timers had said that Major Thornburgh was killed below this hill while leading his men on the march to the Agency. Although I worked most of the hill overlooking the valley, I found nothing. I was hampered in using my metal detector by tall sagebrush and heavy grass.

Since it was getting late in the afternoon I started walking slowly back to my car. It was blowing quite hard and the clouds were forming up, but only a few drops of rain fell. Drove back to Meeker at 4:00 P.M. After supper I completed my notes and read for awhile before turning in.

September 10, 1983 — Was up at 7:30 A.M. and after breakfast, called Aaron Woodward. He had tried to return my previous call but I must have been out. He informed me that he was irrigating the hayfield and I would be unable to get to the monument, dedicated to Meeker, which is located in this field. Perhaps at another time.

Drove to the Meeker marker at roadside, four miles west of town and took more pictures. There is quite a large valley which is called the Powell Valley, and it covers quite a large area along the banks of the White River. Looking south from the roadside marker, one can see a tall metal pole or spire with a round metal ball at the top. This is the spot where Meeker was killed. It is about a mile and a quarter from the historical marker.

I then drove out to the Thornburgh Battle site and crossed the Milk Creek bridge, parking my car at the edge of the barley field. There is a small part which has not been ploughed up and runs along the northern side of Milk Creek. I worked this trip for a few hours but found only one 45-70 cartridge case. I did find a lot of junk items such as old pieces of farm machinery, wire, nails, etc.

Had lunch at 1:00 P.M. and then worked along the south side of Milk Creek, covering the same area as I had covered before lunch, on the north side, however. According to published accounts of the battle, the Indians held this ground and would creep up to within 30 to 40 yards of the soldiers, during the night. But again I came up empty-handed, finding only a few junk items.

During the late afternoon I worked from the dirt road near Milk Creek, heading east, for about half-a-mile, but found nothing. There still remains the north side, heading west, as well as the barley field. These places I hope to cover also. Jeff Squire came along and told me that the threshing outfit that was to do the barley field wouldn't come until Wednesday. I will be leaving on Monday so will have to get to the field on another future trip. I drove back to the motel at 5:00 P.M. and after supper, worked on my day's notes and retired.

September 11, 1983 — Today, I decided to drive out to the Meeker marker west of town. I did so after breakfast and took some color slides of the Powell Valley and the marker. I then drove south and crossed the White River bridge, taking a dirt road to the right, after crossing. One can get an excellent view of the beautiful Powell Valley by driving along this road. This is the valley that Nathan Meeker hoped to plough up and establish farming land for his Ute charges, so they might become self-sustaining. The Utes had been using this to pasture their large pony herd and also had a race track there. Today, most of the valley is taken up by hayfields, while cattle and sheep may be seen in large number. I saw very few horses there, however.

I was able to get some long-range camera shots of the monument which is on the other side of the White River (north side). The monument consists of a tall steel shaft with a large, silver ball, capping the top.

Drove back to Meeker and then out to the Thornburgh Battle site. It was 10:30 A.M. when I arrived there and parked my car near Soldiers' Ridge, where I had previously found many 45-70 cartridge cases. Working until 12:30 P.M., I could find nothing, this time.

Had a leisurely lunch and then decided to work the ridge south of the road, where I had previously found many Henry shell cases, which had been fired by the Indians. After covering about a third of the hill's crest, I started finding cartridge cases again. I found the following:

9 — Henry cartridge cases

6 — unidentified cartridge cases, about an inch

long

I decided to stop work a bit early and drove back to Meeker at 2:00 P.M. It has been a beautiful day with lots of sunshine. Now and then a light wind would come up but would die down again. After supper, I worked on my field notes and read for a while before turning in.

September 12, 1983 — I had an early breakfast and then had the car serviced for my return trip to Greeley. I went to the White River Museum and looked at some of the items there that were associated with the Meeker Massacre. There is a plow there that was used to plow up the land at the Agency. Also the remains of Mrs. Meeker's sewing machine. Pictures of the Meeker family and also a picture of the Ute Chief, Colorow. His pipe is also there. The Museum is located in one of the old army buildings that housed officers and men who were stationed there after the Meeker Massacre.

I also visited the library and returned several books I had checked out previously. I forgot to mention that there was also a picture in the Museum which had been taken on October 9, 1955, showing members of the local historical society, dedicating the monument (the one that is out in the hayfield) to Mr. Meeker.

I left Meeker at 11:15 A.M. and drove to Craig, where I had lunch. I arrived in Greeley at 6:30 P.M. I had covered about 760 miles on this trip.

Trip No. 4

September 21, 1983 — I decided to leave on another research trip to Meeker and left Greeley at 11:50 A.M. It was a beautiful fall day, but a bit on the cool side. As I drove through the Poudre Canyon, it became quite windy. I arrived at Walden at 2:30 P.M. and had my car checked for a gas refill. Drove on to Steamboat Springs and then to Craig.

It was such a beautiful sight as I drove along — to see all of the autumn colors shown by the trees and shrubs. Their beauty would defy a master painter's touch.

After a cup of coffee at Craig, I drove on to Meeker, arriving there at 6:00 P.M. I checked in at the motel and later, went out for supper. I then called Aaron Woodward again to see about getting into the area where the Meeker monument stands. Apparently, he is still irrigating the field so — I'll have to wait. Did some reading and then to bed.

September 22, 1983 — Started the day with an early breakfast and then drove out west of town to take more pictures of the Powell Valley and the Meeker markers at roadside. I then headed out for the Thornburgh site. I parked my car at the western end of the barley field. The barley had been cut but the stubble was fairly high in some spots, making it very difficult to use a metal detector.

My plan was to start at the western end of the field and work towards the eastern end. I judge the length of the field to be about three-quarters to a mile in length and several hundred yards in width. The soldiers' wagon train had been parked at the eastern end, near the southern edge of the field, above Milk Creek. Since the soldiers had retreated over this field area and finally sought shelter in the circled wagon-train, I felt that by gradually covering the lower end of the field I might find some cartridge cases, slugs,

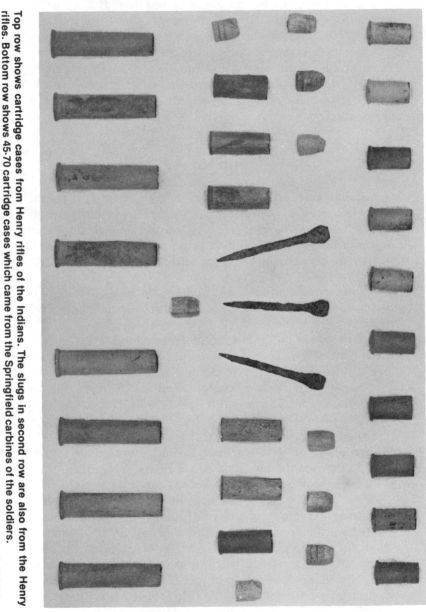

Top row shows cartridge cases from Henry rifles of the Indians. The slugs in second row are also from the Henry rifles. Bottom row shows 45-70 cartridge cases which came from the Springfield carbines of the soldiers.

Photo by Bob Heiser

and other relics of the battle.

I worked steadily eastward, covering a section of from ten to twenty feet wide, along the southern edge of the field. For awhile, I found only pieces of barbed wire, baling wire, nails, and other junk items. Suddenly, at about 11:50 A.M., I got a very strong signal on my metal detector and I joyfully dug up a 45-70 cartridge case! I now knew that I must be nearing the area where the wagon train had been stationed. Looking north, I saw that the high hill where I had found Indian cartridge cases on previous trips, was just opposite of where I was working, and only several hundred yards away.

In the same area, I found the following:

4 — 45-70 cartridge cases
1 — 45-70 slug
9 — square-topped nails

It was now 1:00 o'clock so I went back to the car for lunch and a short rest period. Shortly, I returned to the same spot and continued working till I reached the eastern end of the field. I then worked back towards the western end, covering a swath above the area I had already worked, joined to the eastern end. Nothing else was found, so when I reached the car, I drove back to Meeker.

I visited the library again and checked out several more books. While there, I met a man who is the county assessor. He said if I would stop by at the Court House he would show me an aerial photo of the Thornburgh Battlefield. Had supper and then worked on my field notes before turning in.

September 23, 1983 — After breakfast, I drove out to the Meeker Monument west of town and took a few more color slides. I then drove toward Aaron Woodward's ranch, which is on the north side of White River. Returned to Meeker and went to Court House. The assessor's name is Hartley H. Bloomfield and he showed me some aerial photos of the Thornburgh Battlefield area, as promised. Also a U.S. Geological Survey map of the same area. Bloomfield is a member of the local historical society and knows quite a bit about the Thornburgh Battle.

After a short time I drove out to the battle site again, arriving there at 11:00 A.M. I decided to start work at the same spot where I had found shell cases yesterday and which I believe is the area where the wagon train was parked. Between 11:00 A.M. and 2:00 P.M., I found a number of square-headed nails, pieces of metal and other items.

I worked in this area until 5:00 P.M. but took time out for lunch at 2:00 P.M. By day's end I had found the following items:

                    5 — 45-70 cartridge cases

                    2 — 45-70's, unfired

                    8 — Henry rifle slugs

While I was at the car for my lunch break, it started to rain. It came down in small drops — soft and gentle. It also became a bit windy. However, it cleared up again and I continued working until 5:00 P.M. I then drove back to Meeker and had supper. Worked on notes and read a while before going to bed. I had experienced a very good day.

September 24, 1983 — After an early breakfast, I stopped by at the museum to see if they had found the negative for the monument dedication picture I had mentioned before. They hadn't been able to find it, but will keep looking for it.

Drove out to the Thornburgh site and arrived there about noon. I drove along the road, going east, and stopped at various places to take pictures. I must explain that from this road, which runs along the base of the hills south of it, one can get a good view of the Milk Creek valley below, and the barley field where the soldiers were entrenched within the wagon-train circle.

While I was engaged in picture-taking, I noticed someone out in the barley field with a metal detector. It was one of the men I had met in the library previously by name of Francis McKee. After taking pictures, I parked near the Soldiers Ridge and worked there for a while. McKee drove up and we had a nice visit. He then returned to the barley field and I continued working on the ridge. By 3:00 P.M., I had found the following:

                    4 — 45-70 cartridge cases

                    1 — Henry cartridge case

I then drove to the barley field. McKee had found a flattened-out slug, possibly from a Henry rifle. I worked in the field for a short time but left for Meeker at 5:00 P.M. Had supper, worked on my field notes and then watched the news on TV before I finally turned in.

September 25, 1983 — Was up at my usual time of 7:30 A.M. While I was eating breakfast, Francis McKee came in and visited with me. He told me that in visiting with another fellow he had found out where the location of the soldiers' entrenchment was located. This man claims to have found cartridge cases and other relics there. McKee left for the battle site and said he would look for me when I came out.

From what McKee had told me, I gathered that the soldiers' camp site was substantially the same as where I had found cartridge cases, slugs, nails, and other items. It was the spot in the barley field, about one-half mile from the western end of the field.

A bit later, I drove out to the Thornburgh site and drove along the road which runs above the Milk Creek valley. I could see McKee working at the same spot in the barley field where I had worked previously. I decided to work on the hill just south of the road and across from Soldiers Ridge. I had worked this hill previously and found a number of cartridge cases there. After working for several hours, I had found the following items:

                6 — Henry cartridge cases
                6 — Longer cases, about one inch in length
                1 — Henry slug
                1 — U.S. Army spoon

Walked to the car and had some lunch at 1:00 P.M. I didn't see any trace of McKee. He must have already gone back to Meeker. After lunch, I drove down to the barley field and started working in the area where I believe the soldiers' camp had been. It is so difficult to work in a field that has the cut barley stalks still standing. The closeness of the rows makes it hard to get the metal detector down close enough to the ground to be really effective. My right hand was all scratched up from the stalks. I must wear gloves after this, when working under such conditions.

I only worked for a few hours since it was quite warm and I was growing a bit tired. I had found the following items:

                2 — 45-70 cartridge cases
                1 — 45-70 case — unfired
                1 — Henry slug
                1 — part of a fork
                1 — 1876 dime — what a terrific find!

I was really surprised to find the dime — the first coin I have ever found at a battle site. Hope there are more at this location.

Drove to the Squire Ranch but Bill Squire was not there. I gave his father-in-law a large hacksaw that I had found in the barley field. I then drove to Meeker and after supper, worked on my notes before I retired.

September 26, 1983 — I had decided to leave for Greeley today and packed up my things. After breakfast I went over to the museum. They had a government-published book dated 1879, which contained an account of the Meeker Massacre. I also visited the library and returned one of the books that I had checked out previously.

I left Meeker at 9:50 A.M., bound for Greeley. It was partly cloudy and warm. Drove to Walden where I had some lunch. It was getting a bit windy by now. Continued onward and arrived in

Greeley at 5:00 P.M. I had covered a total of 818 miles on this trip.

I felt that this was a very satisfactory trip. I had found a total of forty-five battlefield relics, had taken four rolls of pictures and slides and had established some important facts about what had happened at the Thornburgh Battle. There are still some missing pieces which I hope to find in order to complete the story of the Meeker Massacre.

Trip No. 5

October 2, 1983 — It was cloudy and cool when I left Greeley at 6:40 A.M. for yet another trip to the Meeker area. I drove to Walden where I had breakfast. It was quite windy and growing colder, by now. It began to rain when I reached Steamboat Springs. It was still raining at Craig and there didn't seem to be any chance that it would stop soon. I had lunch at Craig and then continued on to Meeker.

It was still raining as I checked in at the motel. While waiting for the rain to let up, I watched the Denver Bronco-Chicago Bears football Game. If it stops raining soon, I may still go out to the Thornburgh Battle site, although it has been raining here for some time and it may be too wet to get out into the field.

Went out for supper around 6:00 P.M. The rain had stopped and the sun was shining. Heavy clouds still hung in the skies but they seemed to be scattering. The weather forecast for tomorrow calls for temperatures between 70 and 80 degrees with a twenty percent chance of showers. I turned in for the night at 11:00 P.M., after reading for awhile.

October 3, 1983 — When I looked out of my motel window this morning, I was very disappointed. The clouds had rolled in again and it looked like either rain or snow. I went out for breakfast and sat for a while, trying to make up my mind whether to stay and wait out the weather or to return to Greeley.

I finally decided to check the road going out to the Thornburgh site, to see what condition it was really in. Part of the seventeen-mile stretch is oiled road while the balance is dirt and crushed rock. The road appeared to be O.K., so I continued on out to the site. When I parked the car near the sign at the battle site, it started to rain again, along with a chilling wind. Very reluctantly, I started up the car and headed back for Meeker.

A short distance from Meeker the highway comes to a turnoff which is the road to Buford. The old location of the White River

Indian Agency is about ten miles south, on this very road. I drove to where a sign was posted, which stated that the White River Agency was formerly located in the area below the sign, and on the White River. I plan on contacting the rancher on whose land the former agency was located and get permission to work there. They say there is also an historical marker near the bank of the White River.

The White River at this point runs through a narrow valley, surrounded by high hills. That was the reason Nathan Meeker moved the agency further down-river, where the broad valley, known as Powell Valley, provided ample ground for agricultural purposes.

I drove on to Buford which is only a very small hamlet. Rain was coming down steadily as I turned around and headed back for Meeker. Arrived there at 12:45 P.M. and had my lunch there.

After lunch I stopped by to see Hartley Bloomfield at the Court House. Stopped by at several other places including the library. Finally returned to the motel and decided that unless it cleared up by morning I would return to Greeley. Went out for supper and then spent some in reading and watching TV news before turning in.

October 4, 1983 — What a nice surprise! Not a cloud in sight this morning. It must have been quite cold last night because there was frost on my car. Ate a late, leisurely breakfast, hoping that things would dry out a bit before I drove out to the battle site.

At 10:00 A.M. I decided to give it a try. The dirt road stretch was a bit slippery so I put my Scout in four wheel drive and reached the Thornburgh site without mishap. There was a short stretch of road along the way to Milk Creek that was white muddy. I decided not to risk going any further and parked the car.

I checked the barley field and it was quite soggy and still wet. No chance to work there today but — perhaps tomorrow. I decided to work on several low ridges which are on the north side of Milk Creek and west of the barley field. I reasoned that the Indians would also have held these ridges which are just below the higher hills. They overlook the Milk Creek Valley, up which the soldiers were advancing in their march towards the Agency. My reasoning this time proved to be correct. From 11:00 A.M. to 2:00 P.M. I was kept very busy digging up artifacts. I found the following on the two ridges that I worked:

11 — Henry rifle cartridge cases
1 — 45-70 cartridge case
1 — cartridge case, one-inch long, unidentified

In addition, I found a Henry slug on the bench area above Milk Creek, adjacent to the western edge of the barley field to the area where I had found relics on my previous trips. After digging up a large nail, I gave up — the ground was a sticky, mucky mess.

I took some black and white pictures and then drove back to the dirt road highway. It had dried out somewhat and was much better than it had been in the morning. Drove back to Meeker and went to my motel. I received a phone call from Francis McKee, inviting me to his home for supper. I accepted and drove out to his home, near the edge of town.

After supper, we visited about the Thornburgh Battle and looked at a map which showed the terrain of the battle site. McKee plans to write a book on how to conduct historical research and said he would call on me to perhaps submit a chapter on my research experiences.

I returned to the motel and worked on my field notes. I have heard that the hunters are coming in tomorrow, so will have to see how that will affect my research at the ranch. Perhaps the area where I work is not open to hunters but will have to check with Bill Squire.

October 5, 1983 — I had called Bill Squire last night and he said that the ground in the barley field would probably be dry enough for me to work there today. Had breakfast at 8:00 A.M. after which I drove out to the Thornburgh site. I took a few color pictures and then drove to the Milk Creek bridge where I parked my car.

I walked to the eastern end of the barley field, to the area where the soldiers had been entrenched. It was now 10:45 A.M. and I started work at this spot. Found a few nails, pieces of metal and also the following relics, working until 4:00 P.M.:

> 3 — 45-70 cartridge cases
> 2 — 45-70 cartridge pieces
> 2 — 45-70 shells — unfired
> 6 — Henry rifle slugs
> 1 — 50-70 rifle slug
> 1 — 45-70 slug

My motel reservation at Meeker did not cover tonight's lodging so I drove to the Sleepy Cat Guest Ranch where I had made a reservation. The motel units had no television in them but they were located in a very nice area on the White River.

I had a leisurely supper in the dining room and then returned to my cabin. I spent some time on my notes, did a little reading and then to bed. Will drive to Meeker in the morning for breakfast and then head for home. It has been sort of a mixed-up trip due to the weather but I still accomplished a few things, nevertheless.

October 6, 1983 — When I got up this morning and prepared to go out for breakfast, the windows of my car were covered with a thin layer of frost and ice. I happened to have a snow scraper with me and cleared up all the windows and windshield. I drove in to Meeker where I had breakfast.

I decided to take a different route on my way home this time. I drove south to Rifle, a distance of about 47 miles, where I took Interstate 70, which will take me all the way to Denver. I was slowed down somewhat by road repairs — especially in the Glenwood Springs Canyon. They are putting in a four-lane highway to replace the present two lanes. I was surprised that the Eisenhower Tunnel was only about two miles long — I had thought it was much longer.

The trees along the way were beautiful, all decked out in their multi-colored fall splendor. Traces of snow appeared on all the high mountains along the way. I arrived in Denver at about 12:00 noon and had lunch at a Village Inn Pancake House. Drove on to Greeley, arriving there at about 2:00 P.M. It had warmed up considerably and was an outstanding fall day. I covered a total of 809 miles on this trip.

If the weather holds up I may attempt one more trip to the Meeker area before winter sets in and curtails my research efforts for the time being.

Trip No. 6

October 23, 1983 — The weather reports seem to indicate that there will be good weather for several more days. In light of this, I decided to make one more trip to Meeker. I didn't leave Greeley until 10:10 A.M. What a beautiful day! Not a cloud in sight and lots of sunshine.

I drove to Walden and had lunch there. The wind had now come up but it was still a very nice day. I arrived at Craig at 3:30 P.M. and stopped there for coffee and a little rest. I had played for a benefit dance last night and didn't get to bed until 1:00 A.M.

Drove on to Meeker arriving there at 5:00 P.M. After checking in at the motel I had supper. I then tried to call Aaron Woodward but his wife informed me that he was in Denver on business and wouldn't be home for several days. Also called the Squire Ranch but no one seemed to be at home.

My plans for tomorrow will depend on whether or not I can make contact with the two ranch owners previously mentioned. I went to bed at 11:00 P.M.

October 24, 1983 — It was overcast and cloudy when I looked outside this morning. Had breakfast at 8:00 A.M. and then called the Squire ranch again. Mrs. Squire told me that her husband was out with the hunters. She would have him call me when he came in. Since I didn't know whether or not the hunters would be in the Thornburgh Battle site area, I would have to wait until I heard from Squire.

I decided to drive out towards Buford just to help pass away some time. About seven or eight miles from Meeker, a sign along the side of the road states that this is the location of the former site of the White River Indian Agency. I believe that I mentioned this in one of my earlier accounts.

Turning around, I headed back towards Meeker and decided to drive out to the Thornburgh site. As I neared Yellow Jacket Pass it was misting and a light snow began to fall. I drove on and as I neared the Thornburgh Battle sign, I saw a pickup, stalled in the center of the road. There were two hunters from California, looking for help. Their car had stalled and the battery was too weak to start it again. Since they had a jumper cable with them we connected the two cars with it and got their car started. They were also looking for Bill Squire since they had a permit for an elk but needed to get Squire's permission to hunt on his ranch.

I drove back to the Squire ranch and visited with Mrs. Squire. She was at the Lodge — a building about fifty yards from the ranch house. She promised to have her husband call me when he came in that night. I drove back to the motel and waited for a call from Squire.

Around 3:30 P.M., I decided to drive out to the Squire Ranch again and fortunately, Squire was there. They were getting ready to drive to Craig for dinner. He said it would be O.K. for me to work at the battle site, since no hunting was being done in that particular part of his ranch.

I then drove to the long, low ridge that I call Soldiers' Ridge, and decided to work there. It was getting late in the afternoon and there wasn't much time left for me to work some of the other places. I found only one 45-70 cartridge case and as it was now 5:30 P.M. decided to drive back to town.

Went out for supper and then back to the motel. I worked on my field notes and watched the TV news before turning in.

October 25, 1983 — My hopes for a nice day had been in vain. I

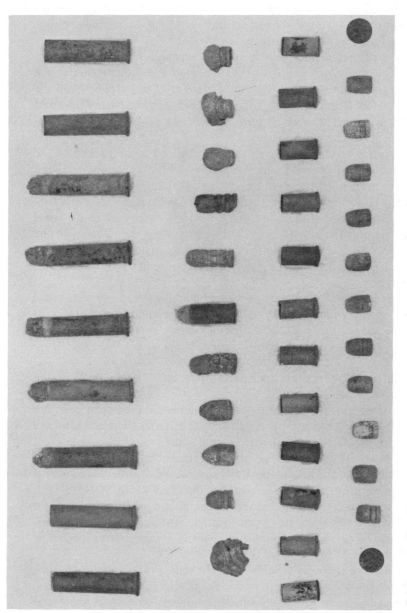

Top row shows 45-70 cartridge cases, some of them unfired. Second row shows slugs from the Henry rifles of the Indians, also several 45-70 slugs, plus an unfired pistol shell. Row three has Henry cartridge cases, while row four shows slugs from Henry rifles. All of these were found at the Thornburgh Battle site.

Photo by Bob Heiser

looked out on a foggy, chilly morning. Had breakfast and then returned to the motel. I debated whether to return to Greeley or wait it out a little while longer. Surely the weather would clear up soon. I decided to drive out to the battle site to see how things looked out there before making a decision.

In driving out to the site, the fog was so low and heavy that I had to turn on my car lights. As I neared the site, the sun broke through for a brief moment, but a blanket of fog still covered the entire Milk Creek valley. I drove to the edge of the barley field and walked towards the eastern end, where the soldiers had been entrenched behind their wagons.

As I was working in this area, I noticed a car parked at the eastern end of the field and a man in a red jacket, metal-detecting in the area north of me. Later on, another man appeared and joined him. They were the men that Bill Squire had previously told me about. They come out from California each year to do some hunting and metal-detecting. They have found many relics at the site, including a cavalry spur. I met with them and we visited for a while. The son, Tom Le Deit, was accompanied by his father, George.

Since it was now noon, I walked back to the car to have some lunch. I had found the following items at the wagon-train site:

1 — 45-70 cartridge case
3 — Henry rifle slugs
1 — button from a soldier's uniform

I also found more nails and pieces of metal — probably from the wagons.

After lunch, I drove to the area where some cattle pens are located and parked the car. Just to the north of these pens are several low hills which are across from some other hills where I had previously found cartridge cases. I reasoned that the Indians probably held the hills on both sides of the small valley. However, I found nothing on these hills and then headed back to Meeker.

I had previously called the owner of the ranch where the old White River Agency had been located, and he had given me permission to drive in to where the historical marker is located. The ranch owner's name is Dan Seely.

I drove through a field for about half-a-mile and reached the sign which was on the bank above White River. The sign or marker, consists of a metal stake with a round ball on top. While I was taking pictures, a cattle-carrier truck drove up. A young man and his wife were in it. He was Mr. Seeley's son and didn't know that I had permission to drive through the field to the monument. We had a nice visit and then they drove off. I returned to Meeker and my motel. After supper I completed my field notes and so to bed.

October 26, 1983 — It turned out to be another beautiful day, but rather chilly in the morning with frost on the car. Had breakfast and then drove out to the Thornburgh site. As I neared the barley field, I noticed that the two men I had met there yesterday, were already there and working in the same area where I had been working.

I decided to work the low ridges to the west of the field. I had worked these ridges previously and found Indian cartridge cases there. The sun was warming things up by now and it felt very good to be warm again. I worked several of the ridges and found more Henry cartridge cases. I also climbed a high hill, which overlooked the ridges where I had been working — but I found nothing there.

I came down from the hill and worked a long ridge which overlooks Milk Creek on the north. I worked this ridge back to where my car was parked, near the Milk Creek bridge, but found nothing more. I had found seven Henry cartridge cases on the low ridges that I had started on.

It was 1:30 P.M. when I returned to the car and had my lunch. I noticed that there were still two cars parked in the barley field, near the spot where the soldiers had been entrenched. I decided to drive there and see what was going on. The Le Deits were busy digging a pit, assisted by a friend from Tennessee. It was unbelievable what they had come up with. Around the edge of the pit was an array of horseshoes, an old army canteen, bones from horses, a large metal hub from a wagon, fragments of charcoal, and a bucket filled with cartridge cases, unfired shells, etc. Strange as it may seem, the pit was located in a spot that I had covered several times before.

George Le Deit said that he was using his earphones with the metal-detector and got a very strong signal at the spot where the wagon train had been located. He and his son Tom, began digging and as they progressed, they unearthed all of the items mentioned. What a marvelous find! I took some pictures and also visited with them for some time.

I finally left and headed back for Meeker. Called Aaron Woodward again but was informed he was still out of town. I drove out to the Meeker historical marker west of town, and snapped a few more pictures. One must take so many pictures to finally come up with a few really good ones — that are fit to use in articles and books.

Returned to the motel and then went out for supper. Have

decided to return home tomorrow. I would really like to stay a few days longer. Will get my things together tonight and leave in the morning.

October 27, 1983 — I left Meeker at 6:15 A.M. It was still dark and quite chilly. I decided to drive to Walden and have breakfast there. I arrived there at 9:15 A.M. It was beginning to warm up by now.

After breakfast I drove on to Ft. Collins. I was slowed up for part of the drive through the Poudre River Canyon. A large hay-truck drove along rather slowly and there was no way to pass him, until I finally reached a passing lane. At Ft. Collins I stopped at the Mall and had a bite to eat. The temperature now stood at eighty degrees.

I drove on to Greeley and arrived there at 1:30 P.M. I had covered a distance of 795 miles on this trip. I was pleased with the progress that I have made in my Meeker research, but felt I need to continue until I can fit a few more missing pieces into the picture — then my story will be complete.

Trip No. 7

June 4, 1984 — I had called Bill Squire, the owner of the ranch on which most of the Thornburgh Battlefield is located and he said there were still some wet spots in the fields, where I would be working. They have had a lot of rain within the last week or so. I decided to take a chance that things would be dried out by the time I got there.

I left Greeley at 6:00 A.M. It was a bit cloudy but otherwise a nice day. Drove to Walden, arriving there at 8:50 A.M. It was now cool and windy there. Had breakfast and also gassed up the car.

Continued onward and arrived at Craig at 11:25 A.M. It was still quite windy, cool and cloudy. Had some coffee at the Village Inn and then resumed my trip. I arrived at the Thornburgh Battlefield exit at 12:50 P.M. and drove on to the entrance of Bill Squire's ranch. The bridge had been washed out so I parked the car and waited. Bill had mentioned he would meet me there between 1:00 and 2:00 P.M.

Bill soon came along with his son Jeff. They had a load of lumber and supplies in the truck as they were going to repair the washed-out bridge. Bill told me that the bridge that crosses Milk Creek had also been washed out. I generally drive over this bridge to reach the field where the soldiers were entrenched in their circled

— 154 —

wagons. There is another way to reach this field. A rancher by name of Doug Wellman, owns the land through which this alternate road runs. Bill suggested that I contact him and get permission to drive over this private road in order to reach the battlefield area.

When I reached the Wellman Ranch, John Wellman, the ranch owner's son, gave me permission to use the road and also gave me instructions how to reach it. I thanked him and then drove over a narrow, deeply-rutted dirt road, after crossing another bridge that also crossed Milk Creek, above where the washed-out bridge was. The road took me to the eastern end of the field. Here I parked the car and walked about a quarter of a mile to where I had worked previously and found both soldier and Indian relics.

It was 2:00 P.M. when I started up my metal detector. Last summer, this field was planted in barley. There were large circles of a tall, thistle-like plant growing in various parts of the field. This made it impossible to use metal detectors in these circles of tall weeds. Now, the thistle-plants were just getting started so I was able to work these areas. I chose to work the circle that was near where I had found shells and slugs last year. This was also near where George and Tom Le Deit found a cache of relics last summer. I worked this circle from 2:00 P.M. to 5:00 P.M., and was kept busy digging up the following artifacts:

8 — 45-70 cartridge cases
2 — Unfired 45-70 cartridges
2 — Unfired 45-70's (upper part only)
1 — Unfired pistol cartridge
1 — Henry cartridge case
1 — Cartridge case (partial) unidentified
2 — 45-70 slugs
1 — 50-70 slug
7 — Henry rifle slugs

I also found at least a dozen of the square-headed nails, used during this period. I am quite certain that this area was the location of the corralled wagon-train of the soldiers. It is the only place in the entire field where any amount of shells have been found. The hills to the north and south are within the range of the Indian rifles, that were trained on the wagon-train below.

During the time I was working, the wind blew quite steadily and the skies were covered with heavy clouds. I left the field at 5:00 P.M. and drove back to Meeker. Checked in at the Gentry Motel and cleaned up. After supper, I worked on my day's notes and went to bed. Hope it will clear up tomorrow so I can take some pictures and slides, as well as continue my research.

June 5, 1984 — It started to rain early in the morning. I could hear it coming down as early as 5:00 A.M. When I finally went out for breakfast at 8:00 A.M., it was still raining. I kept hoping it would stop and the sun come out to dry things out. Perhaps I could still get out to the battle site for at least part of the day — but no such luck.

I stayed in the motel room and worked on my Meeker manuscript. Had lunch at 12:30 P.M. and then stopped by at The Garrison — a gift shop and book store, located near the White River Museum. Sara Lough, the owner, had stocked some of my books last summer. She gave me a replacement order since her stock was rather depleted.

Went out for a drive and back to the motel for more work on the manuscript. Around 6:00 P.M. it started to rain again which turned into a driving hailstorm. It cleared up again at 7:00 P.M. and the sun came out. There are still many clouds in the sky and it is rather cool.

Had supper and then visited with Hank Komosa, the owner of the motel. He informed me that another front was supposed to come in tomorrow. If it appears to be stormy again, I may go home tomorrow and return to Meeker when the weather is more cooperative. Perhaps in July. Did a little more work on my manuscript before going to bed.

June 6, 1984 — I had planned on leaving for Greeley this morning, if the weather was still unsettled. It was. It had clouded up again during the night and started raining as well. As I got into my car to go out for breakfast, it would not start — the battery was dead. Then I noticed the little dome light in the back of the car was turned on. I had inadvertantly left it on when I parked the car last night.

I checked at the motel office but the owner was not there. His wife told me that he would be back in an hour and would get my car started, using the jumper cables. She loaned me their car to go out to breakfast, since the restaurants were at least five or six blocks from the motel.

Upon my return, the owner hadn't arrived yet. Some men who were doing work on a project in the area, had a room next to mine. Since they had jumper cable, they offered to start my car for me. After the car had been started, Hank Komosa, the motel owner, came back and offered to charge up my car's battery with a charger unit that he had. This was done and everything was in good order again. It was now noon, by the time all of this had transpired.

I went out for lunch and yes, it was still raining. I decided I would spend the rest of the day here and take another chance on it clearing up. If it didn't, I would leave for Greeley, in the morning.

I drove out on the highway that follows the White River, upstream. I had checked the location of the old agency, which is about twelve miles from where Mr. Meeker established the new agency. I stopped at the roadside sign which states that the agency was located on the White River about a quarter of a mile from the sign. I could see the marker from where I stood, on the highway. It is on a high bank above the White River.

Drove back to the motel to work on my manuscript. As I drove back to Meeker, I noticed a small break in the clouds to the west. Hope it clears up so I can spend at least a couple of days out at the Thornburgh Battlefield. I went to the motel and worked for several hours on my Meeker manuscript. Then went out for dinner around 6:00 P.M. It started to rain again and it came down steadily for several hours. It finally stopped around 8:00 P.M. I worked on my notes and then to bed at 10:30 P.M.

June 7, 1984 — I could hear it raining steadily most of the night. When I looked outside in the morning, it was still raining. It appears that I will be forced to give up my outdoors research for this trip and return to Greeley. I tried to check out at the motel at 7:00 A.M. but the office was still locked, so I went out for breakfast.

After breakfast I checked out at the motel and headed for home. You guessed it — it was still raining. In driving over Rabbit Ears Pass, I encountered snow but the highway was still clear, although very wet. Arrived at Walden at 11:30 A.M. where I gassed up the car. It was cold and windy here. The rain was a bit lighter but continued, nevertheless.

I arrived in Greeley at 2:30 P.M. It was cloudy with some showers. I had covered a total of 674 miles on this rather disappointing trip, from the standpoint of things accomplished. I will return again to the Meeker area when the weather is more favorable.

Trip No. 8

July 5, 1984 — On this trip, I left my place and drove over to pick up Arlen Horn, who was to accompany me. Arlen is quite interested in my research and offered to go along and assist me in conducting my research at the Thornburgh site. We got underway at 6:45 A.M. We stopped at Walden for breakfast. It was a beautiful, July day.

We stopped at Craig for lunch and then continued onward, arriving at Meeker about 2:00 P.M. We checked in at the Gentry Motel and got some gas for the car before heading out for the Thornburgh Battle site. Since the Milk Creek bridge was still out, I had called the Wellman Ranch and gotten permission to drive through their ranch in order to reach the research site. The dirt road was very rough and filled with deep ruts. We drove through part of the barley field in order to reach the area where the wagon train of the soldiers had been located.

I started my metal detector while Arlen began digging a trench near the spot where the Le Deit's had made their wonderful find, last fall. It was a very hot day and the ground had dried out, with the surface being "hard as a brick." As I worked with my detector in the area where Arlen was digging, I found the following:

4 — 45-70 cartridge cases
1 — 45-70 cartridge case — unfired
9 — Henry slugs — some badly out of shape
2 — Small brass buttons — from an army shirt

Although Arlen worked diligently and sweated profusely in the hot July Sun, we found nothing in the trenches that he dug. I would run my detector over the dirt as he piled it up around the small pits that he dug. I am satisfied there is a great deal still below the surface but we just haven't found the right location. Perhaps we will have better luck tomorrow.

We stopped work about 6:45 P.M. and headed back for town. After supper, I worked on my notes while Arlen watched TV. We discussed our results for the day and decided that tomorrow, we would dig near the area where I had found the artifacts — perhaps we would have better luck.

July 6, 1984 — We were up early in the morning. We wanted to get out to the Thornburgh Battlefield to work while it was still cool. Yesterday afternoon had been so hot that it was difficult to dig for very long in the hard soil. I was told that it hadn't rained since my trip there in early June.

After breakfast we drove out to the battle site. I took a number of color slides as well as black and white pictures, from the road. This included the monument, barley field, Thornburgh Mountain and other points of interest at the site. Then we drove through the Wellman Ranch and through the barley field to the battle site. Arlen started digging another trench at a selected site while I worked close with my detector. I would come up from time to time

George (left) and Tom (right) Le Deit, with relics found at the Thornburgh Battle site. Some of the items shown are: part of a cavalry boot, canteen, wagon wheel hub, horseshoes, etc. Many cartridge cases were also found in this dig, plus some bones from horses. This is the area in which Major Thornburgh's troops were besieged by the Ute Indians.

Photo by Author

and check the dirt Arlen had thrown up around the trench to see if there were any artifacts, in this dirt.

We became quite excited when Arlen found a part of a soldier's boot — but that was all. He did find a piece of wood, also. By now it was getting very warm again and the fleas and horseflies bothered us constantly. Arlen dug three short trenches, at least three to four feet deep. The upper crust of the soil was very hard while the soil further down was rather gummy. I did find the following relics, in the area where Arlen was digging:

> 3 — Henry slugs
> 1 — 45-70 cartridge case
> 1 — Top part of an unfired 45-70 case
> 1 — Smaller cartridge case — bottom part

We decided to quit work about 12:30 P.M. Instead of having lunch at the car we decided to drive in to Meeker and have lunch there. We had our lunch at the Cowboy Corral and then decided to drive out to the White River bridge about a block from town. Arlen caught a nice rainbow on a worm. We then went back to the motel where we cleaned up and had a shower.

We drove to the Sleeping Cat Guest Ranch for dinner at 6:00 P.M. It is a beautiful place, located on the White River about fifteen miles upriver from Meeker. After dinner we returned to the motel. Our plans for tomorrow call for working until about noon and then returning to Greeley. We turned in at 10:30 P.M. — very tired from our day's activities.

July 7, 1984 — We went out for breakfast at 7:00 A.M. It was partly cloudy and much cooler than the past two days. We then loaded up the car and headed for the Thornburgh Battlefield, after checking out at the motel office. We are still undecided as to whether or not we want to continue with our digging at the wagon-train site. It hasn't rained here since my last trip, as I mentioned previously and the ground is absolutely baked to a brick-like material.

We decided to stop at the Squire Ranch, before leaving for home. Bill and his son Jeff were working on some farm equipment and we visited briefly with them. Bill invited us to look at his private lake, which is just a short distance from the ranch — possibly about a half-mile. I also took some pictures of the wagon wheel hub which had been found at the battle site by Tom and George Le Deit, last fall. We drove to the lake which is in a very beautiful setting. While Arlen started fishing, I climbed the high hill above the lake, from where I took pictures of Thornburgh Mountain and the battlefield.

Arlen caught two nice rainbow trout and then we drove to the battle site. I finished my roll of color film and then we decided to leave for Greeley since most of the morning was already gone, and we had planned to leave at noon anyway. We followed the dirt road to the Interstate which saved us at least fifteen or twenty miles from the route that we had previously taken. (We generally drove back to Meeker and then on the Interstate to Craig). We stopped at Walden for gas and also had some lunch. We continued our trip and drove through the Poudre Canyon which was quite busy — with weekenders camping and fishing, in the canyon area.

We reached Greeley at 4:30 P.M. and I said goodbye to Arlen. He had performed yeoman service in digging at the battle site. Bill Squire had told me he was going to "rip" cultivate the barley field, later on this summer. I may go back at that time, since it will be a good time to look for more artifacts at the site.

We covered 692 miles on this trip. I felt it was a very successful one and the relics found there will contribute to the total story of the battle fought there.

Trip No. 9

August 27, 1984 — I had loaded up my car the night before and was all ready to go the next morning. I left Greeley at 6:35 A.M., on a clear, sunshiny day. I stopped at Ft. Collins for breakfast. I then continued on to Walden where it had become quite windy, although it was still a beautiful day.

I passed through Steamboat Springs at 11:00 A.M. and then drove on to Craig where I stopped for lunch. As I resumed my trip towards Meeker, I took the access road which is a dirt road and leads to the Thornburg Battle site. From the cutoff to the battle site is only about twelve miles and is closer than if I had driven my usual route.

It was quite warm by now and getting cloudy as well. When I arrived at the battle site I drove out across the barley field to the spot where the soldiers had corralled their supply wagons and where they were under siege for seven days by the Ute Indians. I used my metal detector in the same area where I had found so many cartridge cases and slugs in the past. From 1:30 to 4:30 P.M., I found the following:

3 — 45-70 cartridge cases

1 — 45-70 shell, unfired (upper half only)

1 — Henry slug

I also found numerous square-headed nails and metal pieces, no doubt coming from the wagons.

I was looking over the area where Don and George Le Deit made their great find last fall. Also where I and Arlen Horn had dug a number of short trenches on our trip there in July. Will decide where to dig tomorrow. A large part of the area where I would like to dig is covered with waist-high thorny weeds.

I had been unable to get a reservation at the Meeker Motels so I drove out to the Sleepy Cat Guest Ranch which is about fifteen miles upriver from Meeker and stayed there. I do have a reservation at the Gentry Motor Lodge for the balance of my stay, beginning tomorrow night.

August 28, 1984 — After a good night's rest I drove in to Meeker for breakfast. I then drove out to the Wellman Ranch to see if I could get permission to work on the hills south of the Milk Creek area and which are on the Wellman Ranch. When I arrived at the ranch, Mrs. Wellman was there and said it would be O.K. to work in the area that I have mentioned. The Le Deits had given me some color prints which they had taken of some Indian forts that were on top of the large hill, south of Milk Creek. Apparently, the Utes had used these forts during the Thornburgh Battle and could fire on the corralled wagon train from this vantage point.

I then drove back on the dirt road to the west end of the hill and after parking my car, started the steep climb up the hill. The hill was covered with heavy underbrush, making my upward progress slow and at times difficult. I had no trouble finding the Indian forts after I reached the top. There were about four of them, along the crest of the hill. They were circular in nature and made up of large rocks stacked neatly to a height of several feet. From the forts, the Utes could fire down upon the embattled soldiers without much risk to themselves. The distance was between 800 to 1,000 yards.

It was very hot but drifting clouds and a slight breeze made it more bearable. I took many black and white as well as some color photos of the forts — also some photos of the Milk River valley below.

Although I worked diligently all around the forts and beyond, I found nary a shell or slug. The Le Deits have been working this hill for years and have found many cartridge cases as well as unfired shells — mainly Indian shells.

At 1:00 P.M., I slowly came back down the hill and drove the car to the Thornburgh Battle sign. There is a picnic table there and that is where I had my lunch. After lunch, I drove to the Thornburgh Battle site, specifically where the wagons had been corralled. I worked the same area that I worked yesterday and found the following items:

4 — 45-70 cartridge cases
1 — 45-70 unfired shell (upper part only)
1 — Henry slug

I also found assorted pieces of tin and nails. As it was near 5:00 P.M., I drove back to Meeker and checked in at the motel. After supper, I spent some time working on my notes. Tomorrow, I hope to try my hand at digging a trench near where the wagons were corralled during the battle. Some of the artifacts are down deep and I hope to find some of these.

August 29, 1984 — This was the day that I had planned to do some serious digging at the Thornburgh Battle site. Specifically, I planned to dig a small trench near where Tom and George Le Deit had made their good find last fall. Arlen Horn and I had been there in July. He had dug several short trenches but our best find then was part of a cavalrymen's boot.

It was a beautiful day with a forecast however, of it being very hot. After breakfast I drove to the site and began digging. The ground was terribly hard and within a short time I had a large blister on my right hand. By noon, I had dug down about three to three-and-a-half feet. I found several small bones of either a mule or horse along with several cartridge cases. I also found pieces of a broken bottle — dark brown in color.

After lunch I did some metal-detecting in the general vicinity of where the wagons had been corralled. I found some more cartridge cases, slugs, and nails. I also did a little more digging at the trench but it was so hot and the ground so hard that I soon gave up. I continued to metal-detect till about 4:30 P.M. and by that time I had found the following items:

3 — 45-70 cartridge cases
1 — 45-70 shell — unfired
1 — 45-70 case (bottom only)
5 — Henry rifle slugs

I also found more fragments of a glass bottle, several horse bones, nails, and a harness buckle. I took some black and white photos of the pit I had dug and then headed back for Meeker. I plan on doing more digging tomorrow and perhaps climb the steep hill south of Milk Creek, to take some color slides of the Ute Indian forts that I had discovered previously.

August 30, 1984 — I had decided to dig at least one more trench at the Thornburgh Battle site. Yesterday's dig hadn't yielded very much so perhaps another dig at a different spot — but still in the same area where the soldiers had held out in their corralled wagon train.

After breakfast, I drove out to the site arriving there at 9:30 A.M. It was another beautiful day with lots of sunshine but it will probably warm up considerably before the day is over. I began digging another trench after I had covered up the one I had dug yesterday. The new trench was a bit to the left of where the Le Deits had made their good find, last fall. I dug down about three feet but found only some pieces of a bottle and some ashes from a fire, plus small bits of wood. I was disappointed but since the wagon-train area covered quite a large space it would be a lucky stroke to hit a good spot — one that contained a lot of relics of the battle. I used my metal detector to work in the same area where I had been digging and found the following items:

> 1 — 45-70 slug
> 2 — Henry rifle slugs
> 8 — pieces from a broken bottle, dark brown in

color
In addition, I found many nails, bits of metal, parts of a harness, and other items. This is definitely the location of the soldiers' wagon train, where they were besieged by the Ute Indians.

It must have been in the high 80's, because it was a very hot day. I now had two blisters in the palm of my right hand, from digging in the hard ground at the battle site.

I drove back to Meeker at 5:00 P.M. After a refreshing shower, I had dinner and then drove out to Aaron Woodward's ranch. He wasn't at home but his wife told me that he was attending a meeting. Will either call him or drop by again — later on in the evening.

August 31, 1984 — It was very cloudy and on the cool side when I got up in the morning. I called Woodward and he said he would call me in Greeley in a few weeks — as soon as the hay crop had been put up. According to Woodward, outlines of building foundations can still be seen where the White River Agency stood. I must explain that the Agency was located on the present day Woodward Ranch. He also told me that the ditch that Meeker built, with the help of his Ute charges, was still in use but had been somewhat enlarged.

I had decided to climb the high hill which is south of Milk

Creek and directly opposite of the spot in the valley where the soldiers were "holed up" behind their wagons. I had climbed this hill on Tuesday and had taken black and white pictures of the Ute forts that are on the crest of the hill. I decided that I wanted some color slides also, therefore, the decision to make the climb again.

It was a steep, long climb, but I reached the summit of the hill by 10:00 A.M. Clouds were still scattered across the sky and now and then a few raindrops fell. I got some good shots of the forts along with some long-range shots of the Thornburgh Battlefield. I had brought my metal detector along and although I hadn't found anything on Tuesday, I decided to give it another try. I found nothing along the crest of the hill but in the area around the forts I found the following:

3 — Henry rifle cartridge cases
2 — cartridge cases — (long — unidentified)
1 — cartridge case — rather short and wide

These are all from Indian rifles. The target of the Indian riflemen was about 800 to 1,000 yards away — the wagon train in the barley field.

Going down the hill was a lot easier than going up. I made it back to the car at noon and then drove to the soldiers' campsite again. Had lunch and then checked out the trench I had dug yesterday. Only a few old nails were found and since there were no further signals on my detector at the three-foot depth, I decided to cover up the trench — regretfully. I had hoped I would hit a good spot and find some of the things the soldiers left behind them when the siege was finally lifted by General Merritt and his command.

I decided to drive to the ridge which is on the south side of Milk Creek and about a half-mile from where the wagons were corralled. I have found many 45-70 cartridge cases on this ridge in the past. I believe one of the companies held this ridge in a delaying action so that the rest of the command could make a safe retreat to the wagon train.

By now the wind was blowing rather hard, making it difficult to hear the metal detector signal. I found junk items such as pieces of wire, twenty-two caliber shells, etc., but finally did find the following items — all buried very deep in the rocky hillside:

3 — 45-70 cartridge cases

Since it was nearing 4:00 P.M. and the weather was still quite unpleasant, I stopped work and drove back to Meeker. Tomorrow, I hope to do a little fishing in Bill Squire's private lake and then return to Greeley on Sunday morning.

I have found a total of 34 battle relics, not including nails, bones of horses and mules, glass particles, etc. I didn't make the big find but have been fortunate to find many items over a wide area — all of them a part of the battle's story.

September 1, 1984 — It rained steadily most of the night, accompanied by a great deal of thunder. In the morning it was cool and overcast but the rain had stopped. Drove out to the Squire ranch and after a nice visit with Bill and his wife, drove to the lake to do a little fishing. Caught four nice rainbow trout and then drove back to Meeker.

September 2, 1984 — I was up rather early and drove to Craig where I had breakfast. Continued onward and arrived in Greeley at 2:00 P.M. I had covered 844 miles on this trip. Accomplishments of the trip can be summarized as follows:

1. Found 35 battlefield artifacts at the Thornburgh site.

2. Located the Ute Indian forts on top of the high mountain, south of Milk Creek.

3. Took many black and white pictures, color pictures, and also slides.

4. Will return to photograph the site of the White River Agency, which was located on what is now the Aaron Woodward ranch.

All of this additional information and material will be of use in compiling my book on the Meeker Massacre and the Thornburgh Battle.

Trip No. 10

October 4, 1984 — It was raining when I left Greeley at 7:15 A.M. I was leaving for another trip to Meeker, Colorado — the Meeker Massacre and Thornburgh Battle sites, to be specific. Bill Squire, the ranch owner on whose land the Thornburgh site is located, had told me that the barley field had been plowed up and it might be a good time for me to look for artifacts again with my metal detector.

I had breakfast at La Porte, which is a few miles out of Ft. Collins and then headed for Walden. It was raining steadily and there were few cars on the road as I drove through the Poudre Canyon. I arrived at Walden at 10:30 A.M. and stopped there for some gas for the car. It was still cloudy and cold but had stopped raining.

Continuing onward, I arrived at Craig where I had lunch. It had begun raining again but rather lightly. As I approached Meeker, I took the cutoff which leads to the Yellow Jacket Pass. From the cutoff to the Thornburgh site is about twelve miles.

I arrived at the Thornburgh site at 1:40 P.M. and parked my car near the roadside sign — the Thornburgh Battle sign. I could see that the road leading to the barley field was quite muddy and I felt sure that the field was in the same condition. I would be unable to work the area until it had dried out somewhat.

I decided to work the Soldiers' Ridge area which is a low ridge running northwest from the road, for several hundred yards. It was now about 2:00 P.M. The sky was covered with heavy clouds and rain threatened at any time. I worked along the very top of the crest and towards the northernmost end, finding the following items, between 2:00 P.M. and 4:30 P.M.:

8 — 45-70 cartridge cases

The ground was quite wet but most of the cartridge cases were found in a grassy area where the ground was a bit dryer. I then drove back towards Meeker as it had started to rain again. I met Bill Squire near the turnoff to his ranch and we visited for a bit.

I arrived at Meeker at 5:30 P.M. and checked in at the Gentry Motel. It rained quite hard most of the evening but let up at about 8:00 P.M. Worked on my notes and then called it a day.

October 5, 1984 — It was still cloudy when I got up this morning, but the clouds had thinned out somehat and here and there, patches of blue sky showed through. Had a leisurely breakfast and stopped by at the White River Museum. Iva Kendall, the curator, was very helpful to me again. She removed a letter from its mounting in a frame and allowed me to have it duplicated. It was a letter written by Fred Shepard on June 2, 1879, to his father, George L. Shepard, in Greeley. Fred Shepard was working as a carpenter for Mr. Meeker, and was killed along with Meeker and the other employees on September 29, 1879.

Towards noon it showed signs of clearing up so I drove out to the Thornburgh Battle site. I chose to work on the hill, south of the road which is overlooking Soldiers' Ridge. After working from 1:00 P.M. to 3:00 P.M., I had found the following items:

5 — Henry cartridge cases

1 — 45-70 cartridge case

1 — cartridge case, about one inch in length

I then crossed over to Soldiers' Ridge and worked there until 4:00 P.M., but found no additional items. As heavy black clouds were rolling in from the north, I decided it would be best to leave for Meeker. I had had some trouble with my Garrett detector and checked the batteries. I replaced four of the nine-volt batteries and will check out the detector in the field tomorrow.

Decided to drive to the Sleepy Cat Guest Ranch for supper. It

Another photo of the "good find" by George and Tom Le Deit at the Thornburgh Battle site. Items are wagon wheel hub, sets of extra horseshoes, canteen, part of cavalryman's boot, and bones of horses.

Photo by Author

was raining again and continued all the way to the restaurant, accompanied by lightning and heavy thunder. Drove back to the motel after dinner and worked on my field notes. Hope tomorrow will be a good day and the ground dried out enough so I can work out in the barley-field area. This field has been "rip" ploughed and there may be some relics that have been plowed to the surface.

October 6, 1984 — I was pleasantly surprised to see that skies had cleared and it would be a day on which the sun would shine, once again. I ate a leisurely breakfast because I wanted things to dry out a bit at the battle site, before I started working there. The newly-plowed field, where the soldiers had been holed up behind their wagons, would need some "drying out" before I could get into it.

It was after 9:00 A.M. when I finally drove out to the site. I put the car into four-wheel drive since the dirt road leading to the field was still very wet, mucky and slippery. I slowly drove down to the Milk Creek bridge and parked the car there. A large pool of water in the road ahead helped me make this decision. I walked about a half-mile to the other end of the field and started my metal detector at 10:00 A.M.

The ground was still quite wet but drying out fast. I worked in the general area where the wagons had been parked and found at least thirty junk items — nails, nuts and bolts, pieces of metal and wire, and also pieces of glass. I also found the following items:

1 — 50-70 slug

1 — 45-70 slug

Returned to the car at 12:00 noon and had lunch. Since I had an appointment with Aaron Woodward at 2:00 P.M., I then left for Meeker. I drove out to Woodward's ranch which is about four miles west of Meeker. Powell Park, where the White River Indian Agency was located, is now all part of the Woodward Ranch.

Woodward took me out to the site of the former location of the agency buildings. He pointed out several ridges and also one that was in the form of a square. These he believes are the places where the agency buildings once stood. A tall metal pole with a metal ball at the top, stands near these ridges and is supposed to be the spot where Meeker fell on that tragic day, September 29, 1879.

I took numerous pictures and then we drove to the White River, which is about 600 yards south of the monument. The native grass which still grows in this area provides more nutrition than regular hay, according to Woodward. We then returned to the ranch house where we visited for a while before I drove back to Meeker. Hope my pictures turn out well. It was a clear, sunny day

— ideal for picture-taking.

October 7, 1984 — It was rather cloudy and cool this morning. However, weather predictions are that it will be a warm day. I had a late breakfast and then headed out for the Thornburgh Battle site. Much to my surprise, there was a car parked near the barley field and a man was out in the field with a metal detector — in fact, he was working in the same area where I had worked yesterday.

I decided to work the ridges that slope towards Milk Creek, from the North. Having worked these previously, I found Indian cartridge cases, mainly from Henry rifles. These ridges furnished excellent cover for the Indians as they forced the soldiers to retreat and seek cover in their corralled supply wagons about a half-mile to the east.

I worked several ridges and from 10:30 A.M. to 2:00 P.M., found the following items:

    13 — Henry cartridge cases

    1 — Henry slug

    1 — 45-70 cartridge case

    1 — Unidentified cartridge case, about 1'' in length

Returned to the car for a bite to eat and rested for a bit. The man that I had observed earlier in the day, was still working in the barley field. In talking to Bill Squire later, he informed that the man was a teacher from Mesa College and had been there several times previously.

Returned to Meeker at 4:00 P.M. Later on in the evening, Francis McKee, who lives in Meeker, stopped by to visit with me. He is working on a book which he hopes to publish, sometime soon. It will be a book on how to carry on research.

October 8, 1984 — I was up at my usual time and had breakfast. This was the day that I had decided to work in the barley field. It was a bit cool but gradually warmed up so that when I reached the field it was warm enough to work without a jacket.

I worked in the area where the soldiers' had been besieged. The ground showed evidence of someone having worked there recently. This was the area where the man from Mesa College worked, all day yesterday. Between 10:00 A.M. and 12:00 noon, I found only the following:

    1 — cartridge case, from an army pistol

    1 — 45-70 cartridge case

    1 — 45-70 case — upper part only

In my opinion, most of the surface (or near the surface) items have been found in the area where the wagons were corralled. Any further finds will involve some deeper digging and excavations. I am convinced that there is still much below the ground, waiting to be discovered.

I decided to call it a day and went to the car for lunch. Bill Squire had invited me to do some fishing again in his private lake. I spend several hours fishing and relaxing at the lake before driving back to Meeker. Had been invited to the McKees' for dinner so I went there after cleaning up at the motel. After dinner, I visited with McKee about his projected book on how to conduct research. I then returned to the motel.

I have made a total of ten trips to the Thornburgh and Meeker sites and feel I have enough material, in depth, to work towards the completion of my book. It's been a very rewarding experience but has also involved many hours of hard work.

October 9, 1984 — It was cloudy and cool when I left Meeker at 8:20 in the morning. I decided to drive by way of the Thornburgh Battle site road and then on to the Interstate connection, about twelve miles beyond the site. I stopped at Walden to gas up the car and also for some lunch.

I had to drive through a very dense fog between Steamboat Springs and Walden. After lunch, I continued on to La Porte where I stopped for coffee. It was now considerably warmer although a bit on the breezy side. The drive through the Poudre Canyon was a very impressive one. Autumn had turned many of the leaves on shrubs and trees into beautiful golden colors.

Arrived in Greeley at 3:15 P.M. I had covered a total of 768 miles on this trip. I had also found a total of thirty-six battlefield relics, not to mention countless nails and other items. I had also obtained a copy of a letter written by Fred Shepard to his father in June 1879. Fred was a young carpenter on Meeker's staff and was killed, along with Meeker and the other agency employees on that fateful day — September 29, 1879.

Most importantly, I also visited the area where the Massacre actually took place, through the courtesy of Aaron Woodward, the owner of the ranch on which the Agency was formerly located. This also makes the tenth trip that I have made to Meeker to do research for a book on the Meeker Massacre.

I have found a total of 346 cartridge cases, slugs, army buttons, and other items — all a part of the Thornburgh Battle. Places where the cartridge cases were found have helped to establish where the Indian positions were located as well as those of the soldiers. A map will show where these respective positions were located and will help the reader to visualize where the action took place.